Richard Hooker

Ecclesiastical Polity: Selections

*edited with an introduction
by Arthur Pollard*

Fyfield Books

First published in Great Britain 1990 by
Carcanet Press Limited
208-212 Corn Exchange Buildings
Manchester M4 3BQ

British Library Cataloguing in Publication Data
Hooker, Richard, *1553 or '54-1600*
  Ecclesiastical polity: selections.
  1. Church of England. Apologetic works
  I. Title
  230.3

  ISBN 0-85635-860-6

The publisher acknowledges financial assistance
from the Arts Council of Great Britain

Typeset in 10pt Palatino by Bryan Williamson, Darwen
Printed and bound in England by SRP Ltd, Exeter

Contents

ACKNOWLEDGEMENT

Text and references are taken from the edition by John Keble, as revised by R.W. Church and Francis Paget (Oxford, 1888).

Introduction

Never surely has a work so noble as the *Laws of Ecclesiastical Polity* emerged from what in one of his impatient moments Hooker called "this tedious controversy". Certainly there is much in the *Ecclesiastical Polity* to bring *odium theologicum* to mind, but the last impression that it leaves is very positive, the application of a fine intellect to a serious problem.

Richard Hooker was born in Exeter in 1553 or 1554, educated there and at Corpus Christi College, Oxford, where he became and remained a fellow until called to the task out of which issued his great treatise. That calling was to become Master of the Temple in 1584, effectively chaplain to the luminaries, present and future, of the legal profession. It was a post of immense importance, not merely in its immediate circumstances but in the general religious conditions of the time. He resigned this post to become vicar of Bishopsbourne (Kent), where he died in 1600. There is little else that we know about Hooker, beyond the much-mooted account of his marriage, judicious or less so according to differing critics' points of view.

Hooker became Master of the Temple with Walter Travers, the deputy, already in post. The latter was a committed Puritan, anxious to take the Church of England further on its way from Rome than it had travelled hitherto. In this he was at one with an influential group of clerics, many of whom, at least in the older generation, had imbibed Calvinistic ideas of doctrine and church government during their exile in Mary's reign (1553-8) in such places as Frankfurt, Strasbourg and Geneva. The moderate reforms in liturgy and church order on which the so-called Elizabethan Settlement had set its seal in 1559 did not satisfy this large dissentient minority, who sustained their agitation to the end of the sixteenth century and whose successors had a brief and illegitimate triumph in the years of Cromwell's usurpation.

Puritan ideas embraced government, doctrine and ceremonial. As early as 1563 there had been an attack in the Convention of that year on the observance of saints' days, the sign of the cross in baptism and the custom of kneeling to receive the elements at Communion, all of which were regarded as relics of Romish practice. In later years controversy extended to doctrine, notably in a famous exchange between Archbishop Whitgift and Thomas Cartwright, whose writings Hooker constantly had in mind. Finally, in 1584-5 the pro-Puritan House of Commons launched an assault on the authority of the bishops. Elizabeth recognized the danger of "no bishops, no monarch". With Whitgift, she acted decisively to regulate worship and to require ecclesiastical obedience. It was, of course, at that very time that Hooker had arrived at the Temple – to find Travers propagating the selfsame ideas that represented such a threat to the Church of England.

The way of the moderate is always difficult. To reform somewhat is never enough for the radical; if reform is necessary at all, why not go the whole length? To reform somewhat is always too much for the traditionalist; he fears destruction in the course of change. The radical sees all bad, the traditionalist all good. Hooker nevertheless steadfastly pursued the middle way. Given that the assault came from the radicals, he had not only to justify the changes from previous Roman practice but also to defend what had not been altered. In terms of rites, ceremonial, liturgy and doctrine this is what occupies him supremely in the great Fifth Book (1597).

But Hooker with his probing intellect saw that it was not sufficient to argue on the level of liturgy and doctrine alone. One has to ask why. What are the first principles underlying the whole question? He therefore starts with the idea of law, beginning with the position that all originates from God. He is perfection and gives perfection to all else. "God therefore is a law both to himself and to all other things besides" (I.ii.3).[1] Next, Hooker had to discuss how man understood and responded to God's law. This latter was revealed in Scripture on which the Puritans placed so much reliance, but Scripture was not all-sufficient. God has endowed man with the faculty of reason, and it is his emphasis

1   Roman capitals indicate the Book of *Ecclesiastical Polity* referred to, roman lower case the chapter and arabic numerals the section.

on this that places Hooker in the central tradition of Christian humanism. Not for him the extreme Calvinism of total human depravity. Thus his enlightened and illuminating excursion into psychology to consider will and appetite, conscience and reason – "The object of Appetite is whatsoever sensible good may be wished for; the object of Will is whatsoever good which Reason doth lead us to seek" (I.vii.3).

In the next three much shorter books Hooker deals first in Books II and III with the excessively literal Puritan insistence on the all-sufficiency of Scripture as "the only rule of all things" (Book II, Title), in the course of which he neatly points out that the Puritans' own selection, arrangement and emphasis on the passages of Scripture they cite is itself an act of reason. In Book IV Hooker defends those Anglican liturgical practices which had been taken over from Rome as being not Romish but universal to the whole Church of Christ.

He is ready now for the climactic statement of his *apologia*. Much longer than any of the other books, the Fifth is full of Hooker's own reasoned but none the less fervent conviction about the rightness and propriety of the Anglican liturgy. Though he must needs take note of those with whom he is engaged in controversy as, for instance, in the passage on the sign of the cross in baptism, it is not the negative and adversarial but the positive and declarative that impresses as we read. One thinks of the eloquence with which he writes on prayer (V.xxiii) or the vision he provides of Christ and His church (V.lvi.7-8) or, again, in different vein, of his extended treatment of the christological heresies in the context of the essential relationship of the Incarnation and the Eucharist (V.li-liv).

Hooker glories in the simultaneous exaltation and edification of Anglican worship, nowhere better illustrated than in the opening words on prayer:

Between the throne of God in heaven and his Church upon earth here militant if it be so that Angels have their continual intercourse, where should we find the same more verified than in these two ghostly exercises, the one Doctrine, and the other

Prayer? For what is the assembling of the Church to learn, but the receiving of Angels descended from above? What to pray, but the sending of Angels upward? His heavenly aspirations and our holy desires are as so many Angels of intercourse and commerce between God and us. As teaching bringeth us to know that God is our supreme truth; so prayer testifieth that we acknowledge him our sovereign good.

(V.xxiii)

Here is what one might call controlled passion, that special and peculiar ethos which is of the essence of Anglicanism.

Books VI-VIII were not published until the middle of the seventeenth century, VI and VIII in 1648 and VII not till 1662. There have inevitably been questions as to whether they are Hooker's, or at least whether they are as he left them. Book VII in particular has been queried, but there might well be more reason to wonder about Book VI which, declaring in the title that it is to consider lay eldership (a special aspiration of Puritanism), is yet mainly devoted to a discussion of penitence. Were it more about lay elders, it would fit better with its successors which are concerned with episcopacy and the Royal Supremacy, i.e., all three would then be about church government and authority. Thus with these three books Hooker completes his study of the three areas of controversy with the Puritans: doctrine, ceremonial and government.

Theological treatises are not popular, and are seldom easy, reading. The *Ecclesiastical Polity* is lengthy, comprehensive, even exhaustive, but it is never obscure. Hooker's style complements his argument. This latter is relentless but always clear and ordered. The statement of the case is often concluded in long compound but, more usually, complex sentences – "long and pithy", as Thomas Fuller put it in his *Church History of Britain* (1655), "drawing on a whole flock of several clauses before he came to the close of a sentence". They possess at once the sophistication and the clarity that calls Cicero to mind. Yet when he needs to be pithy without being long, Hooker can be so, as in, say, balanced series of questions followed by a brief answer.

Again, he can colour an argument with an apt analogy, some-times indeed borrowed from an adversary and skilfully turned against him. And on such occasions Hooker does not restrain himself from moving from straight and serious argument into neatly modulated irony. Overwhelmingly, however, Hooker pre-fers logic over rhetoric, but that separation is an unreal one, for in his mingling of purity, clarity and passion he calls on rhetoric to permeate his logic – an "English Aristotle set to music", as one critic has described him (D.C. Boughner, "Notes on Hooker's Prose", *Review of English Studies*, Vol.XV, 1939).

In the selection that follows I have sought to stress the positive aspects of the *Ecclesiastical Polity* and, in so doing, I have recog-nized that in the presentation of his argument none can improve on Hooker's own order and clarity. I hope that what emerges will fulfil the claim that I have made for him elsewhere: "Sane, noble, sincere, supremely civilised, Hooker remains worth read-ing for himself; clear, comprehensive, profound, he is necessary reading properly and fully to elucidate his contemporaries" (*Richard Hooker*, 1966, p.37). Nor for them only, for his statement of the Anglican position, of that *via media* between the extremes of Rome and Geneva, both Catholic and Reformed, is as valid today as it was in 1600. It is so both in things like the Eucharist, argued furiously in his time and later, and in others such as the ministry of women argued furiously today. What Hooker has to say both of the one and the other, his argument based firmly on Scripture and tradition, is no less true now than it was then. "He being dead, yet speaketh".

Select Bibliography

(Place of publication London, unless stated otherwise)

COLLECTED EDITIONS

Works, ed. with an account of his...life and...death...by J. Gauden. 2 pts., 1662.

Works, with Life by I. Walton, 1666.

Works, ed. J. Keble. 3 vols, 1836, rev. ed. by R.W. Church and F. Paget, 3 vols, 1888. Contains long introduction and Walton's *Life*.

Works, ed. W. Speed Hill (Folger Editions), 4 vols, Cambridge, Mass., 1977-82.

SEPARATE WORKS

Of the Laws of Ecclesiastical Polity. 8 books (1593-1662).

— Books I-IV, 1593; V, 1597; Books I-V, ed. R. Bayne. 2 vols. (with the *Sermon on the Certainty of Faith and the Discourse of Justification*) 1907, revd., 1954 with an introduction by C. Morris; VI and VIII, 1648; VII, 1662 in the *Works*, ed J. Gauden.

Of the Laws of Ecclesiastical Polity, ed. A.S. McGrade, Cambridge, 1989.

CRITICAL AND BIOGRAPHICAL STUDIES

T. Fuller, *Church-History of Britain*, 1655.

I. Walton, *Lives*, 1670; ed. G. Saintsbury, 1927.

R.W. Church, *Introduction and Text of Book I of Hooker's Treatise of the Laws of Ecclesiastical Polity*, 1866.

F. Paget, *Introduction to the Fifth Book of Hooker's Treatise of the Laws of Ecclesiastical Polity*, Oxford, 1899; revd., 1907.

E. Dowden, *Puritan and Anglican*, 1900.

W.H. Frere, *The English Church in the Reigns of Elizabeth and James I (1558-1625)*, 1904.

L.S. Thornton, *Richard Hooker: A Study of his Theology*, 1924.

A.F. Scott Pearson, *Thomas Cartwright and Elizabethan Puritanism*, Cambridge, 1925.

F.J. Hearnshaw (ed.), *The Social and Political Ideas of Some Great Thinkers of the Sixteenth and Seventeenth Centuries*, 1926 – contains "Richard Hooker" by N. Sykes.

S.W. Allen, *A History of Political Thought in the 16th Century*, 1928.

D.C. Boughner, "Notes on Hooker's Prose". *Review of English Studies*, Vol.XV, 1939, pp.194-200.

C.J. Sisson, *The Judicious Marriage of Mr Hooker*, Cambridge, 1940.

C.W. Dugmore, *Eucharistic Doctrine from Hooker to Waterland*, 1942.

F.J. Shirley, *Richard Hooker and Contemporary Political Ideas*, 1949.

P. Munz, *The Place of Hooker in the History of Thought*, 1952.

C. Morris, *Political Thought in England from Tyndale to Hooker*, 1953.

V.J.K. Brook, *Whitgift and the English Church*, 1957.

C.H. & K. George, *The Protestant Mind of the English Reformation 1570-1640*, Princeton, 1961.

J.S. Marshall, *Hooker and the Anglican Tradition*, 1963.

B. Willey, *The English Moralists*, Cambridge, 1964 – contains a chapter on "Humanism and Hooker".

O. Chadwick, *The Reformation*, 1964.

H.R. McAdoo, *The Spirit of Anglicanism: A Survey of Anglican Theological Method in the Seventeenth Century*, 1965.

W. Speed Hill (ed.), *Studies in Richard Hooker*, Cleveland, Ohio, 1972.

A Preface to them that seek
(as they term it) the Reformation of Laws
and Orders Ecclesiastical in the
Church of England

In the Preface Hooker addresses those who wished to carry church reform farther than it had reached by the Elizabethan Settlement. He identifies these men (and in some cases women) as followers of Calvin, the Genevan reformer, as seekers after an alleged purity of church order on New Testament lines and as anti-clerical populists (2). He argues that private judgment must submit to public order (3) and that, where indulged, it leads to dangerous opinions and fantastical self-exaltation (4). The Preface concludes with a plea to the Puritans (5), whom Hooker was addressing, to reconcile themselves to the order of the Church of England.

1   THE OCCASION OF THE WORK

Though for no other cause, yet for this; that posterity may know we have not loosely through silence permitted things to pass away as in a dream, there shall be for men's information extant thus much concerning the present state of the Church of God established amongst us, and their careful endeavour which would have upheld the same. At your hands, beloved in our Lord and Saviour Jesus Christ (for in him the love which we bear unto all that would but seem to be born of him, it is not the sea of your gall and bitterness that shall ever drown), I have no great cause to look for other than the selfsame portion and lot, which your manner hath been hitherto to lay on them that concur not in opinion and sentence with you. But our hope is, that the God of peace shall (notwithstanding man's nature too impatient of contumelious malediction) enable us quietly and even gladly to suffer all things, for that work sake which we covet to perform.

[2] The wonderful zeal and fervour wherewith ye have withstood the received orders of this Church, was the first thing which caused me to enter into consideration, whether (as all your pub-

lished books and writings peremptorily maintain) every Christian man, fearing God, stand bound to join with you for the further-ance of that which ye term the *Lord's Discipline*. Wherein I must plainly confess unto you, that before I examined your sundry declarations in that behalf, it could not settle in my head to think, but that undoubtedly such numbers of otherwise right well affected and most religiously inclined minds had some marvel-lous reasonable inducements, which led them with so great ear-nestness that way. But when once, as near as my slender ability would serve, I had with travail and care performed that part of the Apostle's advice and counsel in such cases, whereby he wil-leth to "try all things" [1 Thes. v.21], and was come at the length so far, that there remained only the other clause to be satisfied, wherein he concludeth that "what good is must be held"; there was in my poor understanding no remedy, but to set down this as my final resolute persuasion: "Surely the present form of church-government which the laws of this land have established is such, as no law of God nor reason of man hath hitherto been alleged of force sufficient to prove they do ill, who to the uttermost of their power withstand the alteration thereof". Contrariwise, "The other, which instead of it we are required to accept, is only by error and misconceit named the ordinance of Jesus Christ, no one proof as yet brought forth whereby it may clearly appear to be so in very deed".

[3] The explication of which two things I have here thought good to offer into your own hands, heartily beseeching you even by the meekness of Jesus Christ, whom I trust ye love; that, as ye tender the peace and quietness of this church, if there be in you that gracious humility which hath ever been the crown and glory of a Christianly-disposed mind, if your own souls, hearts, and consciences (the sound integrity whereof can but hardly stand with the refusal of truth in personal respects) be, as I doubt not but they are, things most dear and precious unto you: let "not the faith which ye have in our Lord Jesus Christ" be blemished "with partialities" [James ii.1]; regard not who it is which speaketh, but weigh only what is spoken. Think not that ye read the words of one who bendeth himself as an adversary

against the truth which ye have already embraced; but the words of one who desireth even to embrace together with you the self-same truth, if it be the truth; and for that cause (for no other, God he knoweth) hath undertaken the burdensome labour of this painful kind of conference. For the plainer access whereunto, let it be lawful for me to rip up to the very bottom, how and by whom your Discipline was planted, at such time as this age we live in began to make first trial thereof.

(Preface, i)

2   SPURIOUS POPULARITY OF PURITANISM

Let the vulgar sort amongst you know, that there is not the least branch of the cause wherein they are so resolute, but to the trial of it a great deal more appertaineth than their conceit doth reach unto. I write not this in disgrace of the simplest that way given, but I would gladly they knew the nature of that cause wherein they think themselves throughly instructed and are not; by means whereof they daily run themselves, without feeling their own hazard, upon the dint of the Apostle's sentence against "evil-speakers as touching things wherein they are ignorant" [Jude 10; 2 Peter ii.12].

[4] If it be granted a thing unlawful for private men, not called into public consultation, to dispute which is the best state of civil polity, (with a desire of bringing in some other kind, than that under which they already live, for of such disputes I take it his meaning was); if it be a thing confessed, that of such questions they cannot determine without rashness, inasmuch as a great part of them consisteth in special circumstances, and for one kind as many reasons may be brought as for another; is there any reason in the world, why they should better judge what kind of regiment ecclesiastical is the fittest? For in the civil state more insight, and in those affairs more experience a great deal must needs be granted them, than in this they can possibly have. When they which write in defence of your discipline and commend it

unto the Highest not in the least cunning manner, are forced notwithstanding to acknowledge, "that with whom the truth is they know not", they are not certain; what certainty or knowledge can the multitude have thereof?

[5] Weigh what doth move the common sort so much to favour this innovation, and it shall soon appear unto you, that the force of particular reasons which for your several opinions are alleged is a thing whereof the multitude never did nor could so consider as to be therewith wholly carried; but certain general inducements are used to make saleable your cause in gross; and when once men have cast a fancy towards it, any slight declaration of specialties will serve to lead forward men's inclinable and prepared minds.

[6] The method of winning the people's affection unto a general liking of "the cause" (for so ye term it) hath been this. First, In the hearing of the multitude, the faults especially of higher callings are ripped up with marvellous exceeding severity and sharpness of reproof; which being oftentimes done begetteth a great good opinion of integrity, zeal, and holiness, to such constant reprovers of sin, as by likelihood would never be so much offended at that which is evil, unless themselves were singularly good.

[7] The next thing hereunto is, to impute all faults and corruptions, wherewith the world aboundeth, unto the kind of ecclesiastical government established. Wherein, as before by reproving faults they purchased unto themselves with the multitude a name to be virtuous; so by finding out this kind of cause they obtain to be judged wise above others: whereas in truth unto the form even of Jewish government, which the Lord himself (they all confess) did establish, with like shew of reason they might impute those faults which the prophets condemn in the governors of that commonwealth, as to the English kind of regiment ecclesiastical, (whereof also God himself though in other sort is author), the stains and blemishes found in our state; which springing from the root of human frailty and corruption, not only are, but have been always more or less, yea and (for any thing we know to the contrary) will be till the world's end complained of, what form of government soever take place.

[8] Having gotten thus much sway in the hearts of men, a third step is to propose their own form of church-government, as the only sovereign remedy of all evils; and to adorn it with all the glorious titles that may be. And the nature, as of men that have sick bodies, so likewise of the people in the crazedness of their minds possessed with dislike and discontentment at things present, is to imagine that any thing, (the virtue whereof they hear commended), would help them; but that most, which they least have tried.

[9] The fourth degree of inducement is by fashioning the very notions and conceits of men's minds in such sort, that when they read the scripture, they may think that every thing soundeth towards the advancement of that discipline, and to the utter disgrace of the contrary. Pythagoras, by bringing up his scholars in the speculative knowledge of numbers, made their conceits therein so strong, that when they came to the contemplation of things natural, they imagined that in every particular thing they even beheld as it were with their eyes, how the elements of number gave essence and being to the works of nature. A thing in reason impossible; which notwithstanding, through their misfashioned preconceit, appeared unto them no less certain, than if nature had written it in the very foreheads of all the creatures of God. When they of the "Family of Love"[1] have it once in their heads, that Christ doth not signify any one person, but a quality whereof many are partakers; that to be "raised" is nothing else but to be regenerated, or endued with the said quality; and that when separation of them which have it from them which have it not is here made, this is "judgment": how plainly do they imagine that the Scripture every where speaketh in the favour of that sect? And assuredly, the very cause which maketh the simple and ignorant to think they even see how the word of God runneth currently on your side, is, that their minds are forestalled and their conceits perverted beforehand, by being taught, that an "elder" doth signify a layman admitted only to the office or rule of government in the Church; a "doctor", one which may

---

1   A Puritan sect which seems to have originated in the Netherlands.

only teach, and neither preach nor administer the Sacraments; a "deacon", one which hath charge of the alms-box, and of nothing else: that the "sceptre", the "rod", the "throne" and "kingdom" of Christ, are a form of regiment, only by pastors, elders, doctors, and deacons; that by mystical resemblance Mount Sion and Jerusalem are the churches which admit, Samaria and Babylon the churches which oppugn the said form of regiment. And in like sort they are taught to apply all things spoken of repairing the walls and decayed parts of the city and temple of God, by Esdras, Nehemias, and the rest; as if purposely the Holy Ghost had therein meant to foresignify, what the authors of Admonitions to the Parliament, of Supplications to the Council, of Petitions to her Majesty, and of such other like writs, should either do or suffer in behalf of this their cause.

[10] From hence they proceed to an higher point, which is the persuading of men credulous and over-capable of such pleasing errors, that it is the special illumination of the Holy Ghost, whereby they discern those things in the word, which others reading yet discern them not. "Dearly beloved", saith St. John, "give not credit unto every spirit" [1 John iv.1]. There are but two ways whereby the Spirit leadeth men into all truth; the one extraordinary, the other common; the one belonging but unto some few, the other extending itself unto all that are of God; the one, that which we call by a special divine excellency Revelation, the other Reason. If the Spirit by such revelation have discovered unto them the secrets of that discipline out of Scripture, they must profess themselves to be all (even men, women, and children) Prophets. Or if reason be the hand which the Spirit hath led them by; forasmuch as persuasions grounded upon reason are either weaker or stronger according to the force of those reasons whereupon the same are grounded, they must every of them from the greatest to the least be able for every several article to shew some special reason as strong as their persuasion therein is earnest. Otherwise how can it be but that some other sinews there are from which that overplus of strength in persuasion doth arise? Most sure it is, that when men's affections do frame their opinions, they are in defence of error more earnest a great deal,

than (for the most part) sound believers in the maintenance of truth apprehended according to the nature of that evidence which scripture yieldeth: which being in some things plain, as in the principles of Christian doctrine; in some things, as in these matters of discipline, more dark and doubtful; frameth correspondently that inward assent which God's most gracious Spirit worketh by it as by his effectual instrument. It is not therefore the fervent earnestness of their persuasion, but the soundness of those reasons whereupon the same is built, which must declare their opinions in these things to have been wrought by the Holy Ghost, and not by the fraud of that evil spirit, which is even in his illusions strong [2 Thess.ii.11].

[11] After that the fancy of the common sort hath once throughly apprehended the Spirit to be author of their persuasion concerning discipline; then is instilled into their hearts, that the same Spirit leading men into this opinion doth thereby seal them to be God's children; and that, as the state of the times now standeth, the most special token to know them that are God's own from others is an earnest affection that way. This hath bred high terms of separation between such and the rest of the world; whereby the one sort are named The brethren, The godly, and so forth; the other, worldlings, time-servers, pleasers of men not of God, with such like.

[12] From hence, they are easily drawn on to think it exceeding necessary, for fear of quenching that good Spirit, to use all means whereby the same may be both strengthened in themselves, and made manifest unto others. This maketh them diligent hearers of such as are known that way to incline; this maketh them eager to take and to seek all occasions of secret conference with such; this maketh them glad to use such as counsellors and directors in all their dealings which are of weight, as contracts, testaments, and the like; this maketh them, through an unweariable desire of receiving instruction from the masters of that company, to cast off the care of those very affairs which do most concern their estate, and to think that then they are like unto Mary, commendable for making choice of the better part. Finally, this is it which maketh them willing to charge, yea, oftentimes even to over-

charge themselves, for such men's sustenance and relief, lest their zeal to the cause should any way be unwitnessed. For what is it which poor beguiled souls will not do through so powerful incitements?

[13] In which respect it is also noted, that most labour hath been bestowed to win and retain towards this cause them whose judgments are commonly weakest by reason of their sex. And although not "women loden with sins", as the apostle Saint Paul speaketh [2 Tim.iii.6], but (as we verily esteem of them for the most part) women propense and inclinable to holiness be otherwise edified in good things, rather than carried away as captives into any kind of sin and evil by such as enter into their houses, with purpose to plant there a zeal and a love towards this kind of discipline: yet some occasion is hereby ministered for men to think, that if the cause which is thus furthered did gain by the soundness of proof whereupon it doth build itself, it would not most busily endeavour to prevail where least ability of judgment is: and therefore, that this so eminent industry in making proselytes more of that sex than of the other groweth, for that they are deemed apter to serve as instruments and helps in the cause. Apter they are through the eagerness of their affection, that maketh them, which way soever they take, diligent in drawing their husbands, children, servants, friends and allies the same way; apter through that natural inclination unto pity, which breedeth in them a greater readiness than in men to be bountiful towards their preachers who suffer want; apter through sundry opportunities, which they especially have, to procure encouragements for their brethren; finally, apter through a singular delight which they take in giving very large and particular intelligence, how all near about them stand affected as concerning the same cause.

[14] But be they women or be they men, if once they have tasted of that cup, let any man of contrary opinion open his mouth to persuade them, they close up their ears, his reasons they weigh not, all is answered with rehearsal of the words of John, " 'We are of God; he that knoweth God heareth us' [1 John iv.6]: as for the rest, ye are of the world; for this world's pomp and vanity it

is that ye speak, and the world, whose ye are, heareth you". Which cloak sitteth no less fit on the back of their cause, than of the Anabaptists, when the dignity, authority and honour of God's magistrate is upheld against them. Shew these eagerly-affected men their inability to judge of such matters; their answer is, "God hath chosen the simple" [1 Cor. i.27]. Convince them of folly, and that so plainly, that very children upbraid them with it; they have their bucklers of like defence: "Christ's own apostle was accounted mad: the best men evermore by the sentence of the world have been judged to be out of their right minds".

[15] When instruction doth them no good, let them feel but the least degree of most mercifully-tempered severity, they fasten on the head of the Lord's vicegerents here on earth whatsoever they any where find uttered against the cruelty of bloodthirsty men, and to themselves they draw all the sentences which scripture hath in the favour of innocency persecuted for the truth; yea, they are of their due and deserved sufferings no less proud, than those ancient disturbers to whom Saint Augustine writeth, saying: "Martyrs rightly so named are they not which suffer for their disorder, and for the ungodly breach they have made of Christian unity, but which for righteousness' sake are persecuted. For Agar also suffered persecution at the hands of Sara, wherein, she which did impose was holy, and she unrighteous which did bear the burden. In like sort, with thieves was the Lord himself crucified; but they, who were matched in the pain which they suffered, were in the cause of their sufferings disjoined".... "If that must needs be the true church which doth endure persecution, and not that which persecuteth, let them ask of the apostle what church Sara did represent, when she held her maid in affliction. For even our mother which is free, the heavenly Jerusalem, that is to say, the true Church of God, was, as he doth affirm, prefigured in that very woman by whom the bondmaid was so sharply handled. Although, if all things be throughly scanned, she did in truth more persecute Sara by proud resistance, than Sara her by severity of punishment" [*Epistles* 50].

[16] These are the paths wherein ye have walked that are of the ordinary sort of men; these are the very steps ye have trodden,

and the manifest degrees whereby ye are of your guides and directors trained up in that school: a custom of inuring your ears with reproof of faults especially in your governors; an use to attribute those faults to the kind of spiritual regiment under which ye live; boldness in warranting the force of their discipline for the cure of all such evils; a slight of framing your conceits to imagine that Scripture every where favoureth that discipline; persuasion that the cause why ye find it in Scripture is the illumination of the Spirit, that the same Spirit is a seal unto you of your nearness unto God, that ye are by all means to nourish and witness it in yourselves, and to strengthen on every side your minds against whatsoever might be of force to withdraw you from it.

IV. Wherefore to come unto you whose judgment is a lantern of direction for all the rest, you that frame thus the people's hearts, not altogether (as I willingly persuade myself) of a politic intent or purpose, but yourselves being first overborne with the weight of greater men's judgments: on your shoulders is laid the burden of upholding the cause by argument. For which purpose sentences out of the word of God ye allege divers: but so, that when the same are discussed, thus it always in a manner falleth out, that what things by virtue thereof ye urge upon us as altogether necessary, are found to be thence collected only by poor and marvellous slight conjectures. I need not give instance in any one sentence so alleged, for that I think the instance in any alleged otherwise a thing not easy to be given. A very strange thing sure it were, that such a discipline as ye speak of should be taught by Christ and his apostles in the word of God, and no church ever have found it out, nor received it till this present time; contrariwise, the government against which ye bend yourselves be observed every where throughout all generations and ages of the Christian world, no church ever perceiving the word of God to be against it. We require you to find out but one church upon the face of the whole earth, that hath been ordered by your discipline, or hath not been ordered by ours, that is to say, by episcopal regiment, sithence the time that the blessed Apostles were here conversant.

[2] Many things out of antiquity ye bring, as if the purest times

of the Church had observed the selfsame orders which you require; and as though your desire were that the churches of old should be patterns for us to follow, and even glasses, wherein we might see the practice of that which by you is gathered out of Scripture. But the truth is, ye mean nothing less. All this is done for fashion's sake only: for ye complain of it as of an injury, that men should be willed to seek for examples and patterns of government in any of those times that have been before. Ye plainly hold, that from the very Apostles' time till this present age, wherein yourselves imagine ye have found out a right pattern of sound discipline, there never was any time safe to be followed....

(Preface, iii.3 – iv.2)

3   PUBLIC ORDER AND PRIVATE CONSCIENCE

... As for the orders which are established, sith equity and reason, the law of nature, God and man, do all favour that which is in being, till orderly judgment of decision be given against it; it is but justice to exact of you, and perverseness in you it should be to deny, thereunto your willing obedience.

[6] Not that I judge it a thing allowable for men to observe those laws which in their hearts they are steadfastly persuaded to be against the law of God: but your persuasion in this case ye are all bound for the time to suspend; and in otherwise doing, ye offend against God by troubling his Church without any just or necessary cause. Be it that there are some reasons inducing you to think hardly of our laws. Are those reasons demonstrative, are they necessary, or but mere probabilities only? An argument necessary and demonstrative is such, as being proposed unto any man and understood, the mind cannot choose but inwardly assent. Any one such reason dischargeth, I grant, the conscience, and setteth it at full liberty. For the public approbation given by the body of this whole church unto those things which are established, doth make it but probable that they are good. And there-

fore unto a necessary proof that they are not good it must give place. But if the skilfullest amongst you can shew that all the books ye have hitherto written be able to afford any one argument of this nature, let the instance be given. As for probabilities, what thing was there ever set down so agreeable with sound reason, but some probable shew against it might be made? Is it meet that when publicly things are received, and have taken place, general obedience thereunto should cease to be exacted, in case this or that private person, led with some probable conceit, should make open protestation, "I Peter or John disallow them, and pronounce them nought?" In which case your answer will be, that concerning the laws of our church, they are not only condemned in the opinion of "a private man, but of thousands", yea and even "of those amongst which divers are in public charge and authority". As though when public consent of the whole hath established any thing, every man's judgment being thereunto compared were not private, howsoever his calling be to some kind of public charge. So that of peace and quietness there is not any way possible, unless the probable voice of every entire society or body politic overrule all private of like nature in the same body. Which thing effectually proveth, that God, being author of peace and not of confusion in the church, must needs be author of those men's peaceable resolutions, who concerning these things have determined with themselves to think and do as the church they are of decreeth, till they see necessary cause enforcing them to the contrary.

(Preface, vi.5-6)

4　CONSEQUENCES OF PRIVATE 'INSPIRATION'

... Herein lieth the greatest danger of all. For whereas the name of divine authority is used to countenance these things, which are not the commandments of God, but your own erroneous collections; on him ye must father whatsoever ye shall afterwards be led, either to do in withstanding the adversaries of your cause, or to think in maintenance of your doings. And what this may be, God doth know. In such kinds of error the mind once imagining itself to seek the execution of God's will, laboureth forthwith to remove both things and persons which any way hinder it from taking place; and in such cases if any strange or new thing seem requisite to be done, a strange and new opinion concerning the lawfulness thereof is withal received and broached under countenance of divine authority.

[6] One example herein may serve for many, to shew that false opinions, touching the will of God to have things done, are wont to bring forth mighty and violent practices against the hindrances of them; and those practices new opinions more pernicious than the first, yea most extremely sometimes opposite to that which the first did seem to intend. Where the people took upon them the reformation of the Church by casting out popish superstition, they having received from their pastors a general instruction "that whatsoever the heavenly Father hath not planted must be rooted out" [Matthew xv.13], proceeded in some foreign places so far that down went oratories and the very temples of God themselves....

[7] From this they proceeded unto public reformation, first ecclesiastical, and then civil. Touching the former, they boldly avouched that themselves only had the truth, which thing upon peril of their lives they would at all times defend; and that since the apostles lived, the same was never before in all points sincerely taught. Wherefore that things might again be brought to that ancient integrity which Jesus Christ by his word requireth, they began to control the ministers of the gospel for attributing so much force and virtue unto the scriptures of God read, whereas the truth was, that when the word is said to engender faith in the heart, and to convert the soul of man, or to work any such spiritual divine effect, these speeches are not thereunto appliable as it is read or preached, but as it is ingrafted in us by the power of the Holy Ghost opening the eyes of our understanding, and so revealing the mysteries of God, according to that which Jeremy promised before should be, saying, "I will put my law in their inward parts, and I will write it in their hearts" [Jeremiah xxi.33].

The Book of God they notwithstanding for the most part so admired, that other disputation against their opinions than only by allegation of Scripture they would not hear; besides it they thought no other writings in the world should be studied; insomuch as one of their great prophets exhorting them to cast away all respects unto human writings, so far to his motion they condescended, that as many as had any books save the Holy Bible in their custody, they brought and set them publicly on fire. When they and their Bibles were alone together, what strange fantastical opinion soever at any time entered into their heads, their use was to think the Spirit taught it them. Their phrensies concerning our Saviour's incarnation, the state of souls departed, and suchlike, are things needless to be rehearsed. And forasmuch as they were of the same suit with those of whom the apostle speaketh, saying, "They are still learning, but never attain to the knowledge of truth" [2 Timothy iii.7], it was no marvel to see them every day broach some new thing, not heard of before. Which restless levity they did interpret to be their growing to spiritual perfection, and a proceeding from faith to faith...

...My purpose herein is to shew, that when the minds of men are once erroneously persuaded that it is the will of God to have those things done which they fancy, their opinions are as thorns in their sides, never suffering them to take rest till they have brought their speculations into practice. The lets and impediments of which practice their restless desire and study to remove leadeth them every day forth by the hand into other more dangerous opinions, sometimes quite and clean contrary to their first pretended meanings: so as what will grow out of such errors as go masked under the cloak of divine authority, impossible it is that ever the wit of man should imagine, till time have brought forth the fruits of them: for which cause it behoveth wisdom to fear the sequels thereof, even beyond all apparent cause of fear.

(Preface, viii.5-6,7,12)

5 FINAL PLEA TO PURITANS

IX. The best and safest way for you therefore, my dear brethren, is, to call your deeds past to a new reckoning, to reexamine the cause ye have taken in hand, and to try it even point by point, argument by argument, with all the diligent exactness ye can; to lay aside the gall of that bitterness wherein your minds have hitherto over-abounded, and with meekness to search the truth. Think ye are men, deem it not impossible for you to err; sift unpartially your own hearts, whether it be force of reason or vehemency of affection, which hath bred and still doth feed these opinions in you. If truth do any where manifest itself, seek not to smother it with glosing delusions, acknowledge the greatness thereof, and think it your best victory when the same doth prevail over you.

[2] That ye have been earnest in speaking or writing again and again the contrary way, shall be no blemish or discredit at all unto you. Amongst so many so huge volumes as the infinite pains of St. Augustine have brought forth, what one hath gotten him greater love, commendation and honour, than the book wherein he carefully collecteth his own oversights, and sincerely condemneth them? Many speeches there are of Job's whereby his wisdom and other virtues may appear; but the glory of an ingenuous mind he hath purchased by these words only, "Behold, I will lay mine hand on my mouth: I have spoken once, yet will I not therefore maintain argument; yea twice, howbeit for that cause further I will not proceed" [Job xl.4-5].

[3] Far more comfort it were for us (so small is the joy we take in these strifes) to labour under the same yoke, as men that look for the same eternal reward of their labours, to be joined with you in bands of indissoluble love and amity, to live as if our persons being many our souls were but one, rather than in such dismembered sort to spend our few and wretched days in a tedious prosecuting of wearisome contentions: the end whereof, if they have not some speedy end, will be heavy even on both sides. Brought already we are even to that estate which Gregory Nazianzen mournfully describeth, saying, "My mind leadeth

me" (sith there is no other remedy) "to fly and to convey myself into some corner out of sight, where I may scape from this cloudy tempest of maliciousness, whereby all parts are entered into a deadly war amongst themselves, and that little remnant of love which was, is now consumed to nothing. The only godliness we glory in, is to find out somewhat whereby we may judge others to be ungodly. Each other's faults we observe as matter of exprobration and not of grief. By these means we are grown hateful in the eyes of the heathens themselves, and (which woundeth us the more deeply) able we are not to deny but that we have deserved their hatred. With the better sort of our own our fame and credit is clean lost. The less we are to marvel if they judge vilely of us, who although we did well would hardly allow thereof. On our backs they also build that are lewd, and what we object one against another, the same they use to the utter scorn and disgrace of us all. This we have gained by our mutual home-dissensions. This we are worthily rewarded with, which are more forward to strive than becometh men of virtuous and mild disposition".

[4] But our trust in the Almighty is, that with us contentions are now at their highest float, and that the day will come (for what cause of despair is there?) when the passions of former enmity being allayed, we shall with ten times redoubled tokens of our unfeignedly reconciled love, shew ourselves each towards other the same which Joseph and the brethren of Joseph were at the time of their interview in Egypt. Our comfortable expectation and most thirsty desire whereof what man soever amongst you shall any way help to satisfy, (as we truly hope there is no one amongst you but some way or other will), the blessings of the God of peace, both in this world and in the world to come, be upon him moe than the stars of the firmament in number.

(Preface, ix)

What Things are handled

in the Books following:

Book the First, concerning Laws in general.

The Second, of the use of Divine Law contained in Scripture; whether that be the only Law which ought to serve for our direction in all things without exception.

The Third, of Laws concerning Ecclesiastical Polity; whether the form thereof be in Scripture so set down, that no addition or change is lawful.

The Fourth, of general exceptions taken against the Laws of our Polity, as being popish, and banished out of certain reformed churches.

The Fifth, of our Laws that concern the public religious duties of the Church, and the manner of bestowing that Power of Order, which enableth men in sundry degrees and callings to execute the same.

The Sixth, of the Power of Jurisdiction, which the reformed platform claimeth unto lay-elders, with others.

The Seventh, of the Power of Jurisdiction, and the honour which is annexed thereunto in Bishops.

The Eighth, of the power of Ecclesiastical Dominion or Supreme Authority, which with us the highest governor or Prince hath, as well in regard of domestical Jurisdictions, as of that other foreignly claimed by the Bishop of Rome.

Book I

In Book I Hooker begins by declaring his intentions in writing. He goes on to ground his argument on law and reason. He posits that God is law and that all His operations are directed to the fulfilment of perfect law, the expression of Himself and the achievement of His purpose (7). Hooker then traces law in nature (8), among the angels and in man's desire for order and perfection (9). This last leads him into the domain of psychology, considering how man comes to recognize goodness which originates in God (10) and the part played in this by the exercise of his will (11). Reason guides the will to discover the laws that embody goodness (12), and observance (or otherwise) of the laws then determines reward or punishment (13). This leads on to a discussion of law within social groupings (14), between nations (15) and in the church (16). This line of argument reaches its climax in chapter xi (17) where Hooker argues that man's happiness, his chief good, lies in communion with God – as derived from the instruction of the Scriptures (18, 19). The book ends with an eulogy of law (20).

6   PROBLEMS OF APOLOGY

I. He that goeth about to persuade a multitude, that they are not so well governed as they ought to be, shall never want attentive and favourable hearers; because they know the manifold defects whereunto every kind of regiment is subject, but the secret lets and difficulties, which in public proceedings are innumerable and inevitable, they have not ordinarily the judgment to consider. And because such as openly reprove supposed disorders of state are taken for principal friends to the common benefit of all, and for men that carry singular freedom of mind; under this fair and plausible colour whatsoever they utter passeth for good and current. That which wanteth in the weight of their speech, is supplied by the aptness of men's minds to accept and believe it. Whereas on the other side, if we maintain things that are established, we have not only to strive with a number of heavy prejudices deeply rooted in the hearts of men, who think that herein we serve the time, and speak in favour of the present state, because thereby we either hold or seek preferment; but also to bear such exceptions as minds so averted beforehand usually take against that which they are loth should be poured into them.

[2] Albeit therefore much of that we are to speak in this present cause may seem to a number perhaps tedious, perhaps obscure, dark, and intricate; (for many talk of the truth, which never sounded the depth from whence it springeth; and therefore when they are led thereunto they are soon weary, as men drawn from those beaten paths wherewith they have been inured); yet this may not so far prevail as to cut off that which the matter itself requireth, howsoever the nice humour of some be therewith pleased or no. They unto whom we shall seem tedious are in no wise injured by us, because it is in their own hands to spare that labour which they are not willing to endure. And if any complain of obscurity, they must consider, that in these matters it cometh no otherwise to pass than in sundry the works both of art and also of nature, where that which hath greatest force in the very things we see is notwithstanding itself oftentimes not seen. The stateliness of houses, the goodliness of trees, when we behold them delighteth the eye; but that foundation which beareth up the one, that root which ministereth unto the other nourishment and life, is in the bosom of the earth concealed; and if there be at any time occasion to search into it, such labour is then more necessary than pleasant, both to them which undertake it and for the lookers-on. In like manner, the use and benefit of good laws all that live under them may enjoy with delight and comfort, albeit the grounds and first original causes from whence they have sprung be unknown, as to the greatest part of men they are. But when they who withdraw their obedience pretend that the laws which they should obey are corrupt and vicious; for better examination of their quality, it behoveth the very foundation and root, the highest wellspring and fountain of them to be discovered. Which because we are not oftentimes accustomed to do, when we do it the pains we take are more needful a great deal than acceptable, and the matters which we handle seem by reason of newness (till the mind grow better acquainted with them) dark, intricate, and unfamiliar. For as much help whereof as may be in this case, I have endeavoured

throughout the body of this whole discourse, that every former part might give strength unto all that follow, and every later bring some light unto all before. So that if the judgments of men do but hold themselves in suspense as touching these first more general meditations, till in order they have perused the rest that ensue; what may seem dark at the first will afterwards be found more plain, even as the later particular decisions will appear I doubt not more strong, when the other have been read before.

[3] The Laws of the Church, whereby for so many ages together we have been guided in the exercise of Christian religion and the service of the true God, our rites, customs, and orders of ecclesiastical government, are called in question: we are accused as men that will not have Christ Jesus to rule over them, but have wilfully cast his statutes behind their backs, hating to be reformed and made subject unto the sceptre of his discipline. Behold therefore we offer the laws whereby we live unto the general trial and judgment of the whole world; heartily beseeching Almighty God, whom we desire to serve according to his own will, that both we and others (all kinds of partial affection being clean laid aside) may have eyes to see and hearts to embrace the things that in his sight are most acceptable.

And because the point about which we strive is the quality of our laws, our first entrance hereinto cannot better be made, than with consideration of the nature of law in general, and of that law which giveth life unto all the rest, which are commendable, just, and good; namely the law whereby the Eternal himself doth work. Proceeding from hence to the law, first of Nature, then of Scripture, we shall have the easier access unto those things which come after to be debated, concerning the particular cause and question which we have in hand.   (I.i)

7   GOD AS LAW

II. All things that are, have some operation not violent or casual. Neither doth any thing ever begin to exercise the same, without some fore-conceived end for which it worketh. And the end which it worketh for is not obtained, unless the work be also fit to obtain it by. For unto every end every operation will not serve. That which doth assign unto each thing the kind, that which doth moderate the force and power, that which doth appoint the form and measure, of working, the same we term a *Law*. So that no certain end could ever be attained, unless the actions whereby it is attained were regular; that is to say, made suitable, fit and correspondent unto their end, by some canon, rule or law. Which thing doth first take place in the works even of God himself.

[2] All things therefore do work after a sort, according to law: all other things according to a law, whereof some superior, unto whom they are subject, is author; only the works and operations of God have Him both for their worker, and for the law whereby they are wrought. The being of God is a kind of law to his working: for that perfection which God is, giveth perfection to that he doth. Those natural, necessary, and internal operations of God, the Generation of the Son, the Proceeding of the Spirit, are without the compass of my present intent: which is to touch only such operations as have their beginning and being by a voluntary purpose, wherewith God hath eternally decreed when and how they should be. Which eternal decree is that we term an eternal law.

Dangerous it were for the feeble brain of man to wade far into the doings of the Most High; whom although to know be life, and joy to make mention of his name; yet our soundest knowledge is to know that we know him not as indeed he is, neither can know him: and our safest eloquence concerning him is our silence, when we confess without confession that his glory is inexplicable, his greatness above our capacity and reach. He is above, and we upon earth; therefore it behoveth our words to be wary and few [Eccles. v.2].

Our God is one, or rather very *Oneness*, and mere unity, having nothing but itself in itself, and not consisting (as all things do besides God) of many things. In which essential Unity of God a Trinity personal nevertheless subsisteth, after a manner far exceeding the possibility of man's conceit. The works which outwardly are of God, they are in such sort of Him being one, that each Person hath in them somewhat peculiar and proper. For being Three, and they all subsisting in the essence of one Deity; from the Father, by the Son, through the Spirit, all things are. That which the Son doth hear of the Father, and which the Spirit doth receive of the Father and the Son, the same we have at the hands of the Spirit as being the last, and therefore the nearest unto us in order, although in power the same with the second and the first. [John xvi.13-15] . . .

[3] . . . God therefore is a law both to himself, and to all other things besides. To himself he is a law in all those things, whereof our Saviour speaketh, saying, "My Father worketh as yet, so I" [John v.17]. God worketh nothing without cause. All those things which are done by him have some end for which they are done; and the end for which they are done is a reason of his will to do them. His will had not inclined to create woman, but that he saw it could not be well if she were not created. *Non est bonum*, "It is not good man should be alone; therefore let us make a helper for him" [Genesis ii.18]. That and nothing else is done by God, which to leave undone were not so good.

If therefore it be demanded, why God having power and ability infinite, the effects notwithstanding of that power are all so limited as we see they are: the reason hereof is the end which he hath proposed, and the law whereby his wisdom hath stinted the effects of his power in such sort, that it doth not work infinitely, but correspondently unto that end for which it worketh, even "all things Χρηστως, in most decent and comely sort", all things in "Measure, Number, and Weight".

[4] The general end of God's external working is the exercise of his most glorious and most abundant virtue. Which abundance doth shew itself in variety, and for that cause this variety is oftentimes in Scripture exprest by the name of *riches* [Eph. i.7; Phil. iv.19; Col. ii.3]. "The Lord hath made all things for his own sake" [Proverbs xvi.4]. Not that any thing is made to be beneficial unto him, but all things for him to shew beneficence and grace in them.

The particular drift of every act proceeding externally from God we are not able to discern, and therefore cannot always give the proper and certain reason of his works. Howbeit undoubtedly a proper and certain reason there is of every finite work of God, inasmuch as there is a law imposed upon it; which if there were not, it should be infinite, even as the worker himself is.

[5] They err therefore who think that of the will of God to do this or that there is no reason besides his will. Many times no reason known to us; but that there is no reason thereof I judge it most unreasonable to imagine, inasmuch as he worketh all things κατὰ τὴν βουλν του θελήματος αυτου, not only according to his own will, but "the Counsel of his own will" [Eph. i.11]. And whatsoever is done with counsel or wise resolution hath of necessity some reason why it should be done, albeit that reason be to us in some things so secret, that it forceth the wit of man to stand, as the blessed Apostle himself doth, amazed thereat: "O the depth of the riches both of the wisdom and knowledge of God! How unsearchable are his judgments," &c. [Romans xi.33]. That law eternal which God himself hath made to himself, and thereby worketh all things whereof he is the cause and author; that law in the admirable frame whereof shineth with most perfect beauty the countenance of that wisdom which hath testified concerning herself, "The Lord possessed me in the beginning of his way, even before his works of old I was set up" [Proverbs viii.22]; that law, which hath been the pattern to make, and is the card to guide the world by; that law which hath been of God and with God everlastingly; that law, the author and observer whereof is one only God to be blessed for ever: how should either men or angels be able perfectly to behold? The book of this law we are neither able nor worthy to open and look into. That little thereof which we darkly apprehend we admire, the rest with religious ignorance we humbly and meekly adore.

[6] Seeing therefore that according to this law He worketh, "of whom, through whom, and for whom, are all things" [Romans xi.36]; although there seem unto us confusion and disorder in the affairs of this present world: "Tamen quoniam bonus mundum rector temperat, recte fieri cuncta ne dubites",[1] "let no man

---

1 Boethius, *Consolations of Philosophy*. IV.5.

doubt but that every thing is well done, because the world is ruled by so good a guide", as transgresseth not His own law, than which nothing can be more absolute, perfect, and just.

The law whereby He worketh is eternal, and therefore can have no show or colour of mutability: for which cause, a part of that law being opened in the promises which God hath made (because his promises are nothing else but declarations what God will do for the good of men) touching those promises the Apostle hath witnessed, that God may as possibly "deny himself" [2 Timothy ii.13] and not be God, as fail to perform them. And concerning the counsel of God, he termeth it likewise a thing "unchangeable" [Hebrews vi.17]; the counsel of God, and that law of God whereof now we speak, being one.

Nor is the freedom of the will of God any whit abated, let or hindered, by means of this; because the imposition of this law upon himself is his own free and voluntary act.

This law therefore we may name eternal, being "that order which God before all ages hath set down with himself, for himself to do all things by".   (I.ii.1-2, 3-6)

8   LAW IN NATURE

III. I am not ignorant that by "law eternal" the learned for the most part do understand the order, not which God hath eternally purposed himself in all his works to observe, but rather that which with himself he hath set down as expedient to be kept by all his creatures, according to the several condition wherewith he hath endued them. They who thus are accustomed to speak apply the name of Law unto that only rule of working which superior authority imposeth; whereas we somewhat more enlarging the sense thereof term any kind of rule or canon, whereby actions are framed, a law. Now that law which, as it is laid up in the bosom of God, they call *Eternal*, receiveth according unto the different kinds of things which are subject unto it different and sundry kinds of names. That part of it which ordereth natural agents we call usually *Nature's* law; that which Angels do clearly behold and without any swerving observe is a law *Celestial* and heavenly; the law of *Reason*, that which bindeth creatures reasonable in this world, and with which by reason that may most plainly perceive themselves bound; that which bindeth them, and is not known but by special revelation from God, *Divine* law; *Human* law, that which out of the law either of reason or of God men probably gathering to be expedient, they make it a law. All things therefore, which are as they ought to be, are conformed unto *this second law eternal*; and even those things which to this eternal law are not conformable are notwithstanding in some sort ordered by *the first eternal law*. For what good or evil is there under the sun, what action correspondent or repugnant unto the law which God hath imposed upon his creatures, but in or upon it God doth work according to the law which himself hath eternally purposed to keep; that is to say, the *first law eternal*? So that a twofold law eternal being thus made, it is not hard to conceive how they both take place in all things.

[2] Wherefore to come to the law of nature: albeit thereby we sometimes mean that manner of working which God hath set for each created thing to keep; yet forasmuch as those things are termed most properly natural agents, which keep the law of their kind unwittingly, as the heavens and elements of the world, which can do no otherwise than they do; and forasmuch as we give unto intellectual natures the name of *Voluntary* agents, that so we may distinguish them from the other; expedient it will be, that we sever the law of nature observed by the one from that which the other is tied unto. Touching the former, their strict keeping of one tenure, statute, and law, is spoken of by all, but hath in it more than men have as yet attained to know, or perhaps ever shall attain, seeing the travail of wading herein is given of God to the sons of men, that perceiving how much the least thing in the world hath in it more than the wisest are able to reach unto, they may by this means learn humility. Moses, in describing the work of creation, attributeth speech unto God: "God said, Let there be light: let there be a firmament: let the waters under the heaven be gathered together into one place: let the earth bring

forth: let there be lights in the firmament of heaven". Was this only the intent of Moses, to signify the infinite greatness of God's power by the easiness of his accomplishing such effects, without travail, pain, or labour? Surely it seemeth that Moses had herein besides this a further purpose, namely, first to teach that God did not work as a necessary but a voluntary agent, intending beforehand and decreeing with himself that which did outwardly proceed from him: secondly, to shew that God did then institute a law natural to be observed by creatures, and therefore according to the manner of laws, the institution thereof is described, as being established by solemn injunction. His commanding those things to be which are, and to be in such sort as they are, to keep that tenure and course which they do, importeth the establishment of nature's law. This world's first creation, and the preservation since of things created, what is it but only so far forth a manifestation by execution, what the eternal law of God is concerning things natural? And as it cometh to pass in a kingdom rightly ordered, that after a law is once published, it presently takes effect far and wide, all states framing themselves thereunto; even so let us think it fareth in the natural course of the world: since the time that God did first proclaim the edicts of his law upon it, heaven and earth have hearkened unto his voice, and their labour hath been to do his will: He "made a law for the rain" [Job xxviii.26]; He gave his "decree unto the sea, that the waters should not pass his commandment" [Jeremiah v.22]. Now if nature should intermit her course, and leave altogether though it were but for a while the observation of her own laws; if those principal and mother elements of the world, whereof all things in this lower world are made, should lose the qualities which now they have; if the frame of that heavenly arch erected over our heads should loosen and dissolve itself; if celestial spheres should forget their wonted motions, and by irregular volubility turn themselves any way as it might happen; if the prince of the lights of heaven, which now as a giant doth run his unwearied course [Psalm xix.5], should as it were through a languishing faintness begin to stand and to rest himself; if the moon should wander from her beaten way, the times and seasons of the year blend themselves by disordered and confused mixture, the winds breathe out their last gasp, the clouds yield no rain, the earth be defeated of heavenly influence, the fruits of the earth pine away as children at the withered breasts of their mother no longer able to yield them relief: what would become of man himself, whom these things now do all serve? See we not plainly that obedience of creatures unto the law of nature is the stay of the whole world?

(I.iii.1-2)

9   HUMAN YEARNING FOR PERFECTION

V. God alone excepted, who actually and everlastingly is whatsoever he may be, and which cannot hereafter be that which now he is not; all other things besides are somewhat in possibility, which as yet they are not in act. And for this cause there is in all things an appetite or desire, whereby they incline to something which they may be; and when they are it, they shall be perfecter than now they are. All which perfections are contained under the general name of Goodness. And because there is not in the world any thing whereby another may not some way be made the perfecter, therefore all things that are, are good....

... The first degree of goodness is that general perfection which all things do seek, in desiring the continuance of their being. All things therefore coveting as much as may be to be like unto God in being ever, that which cannot hereunto attain personally doth seek to continue itself another way, that is by offspring and propagation. The next degree of goodness is that which each thing coveteth by affecting resemblance with God in the constance and excellency of those operations which belong unto their kind. The immutability of God they strive unto, by working either always or for the most part after one and the same manner; his absolute exactness they imitate, by tending unto that which is most exquisite in every particular. Hence have risen a number of axioms in philosophy, showing how "the works of nature do always aim at that which cannot be bettered".

[2] Again, sith there can be no goodness desired which proceedeth not from God himself, as from the supreme cause of all things; and every effect doth after a sort contain, at leastwise resemble, the cause from which it proceedeth: all things in the world are said in some sort to seek the highest, and to covet more or less the participation of God himself. Yet this doth no where so much appear as it doth in man, because there are so many kinds of perfections which man seeketh.   (I.v.1-2)

10   GRADUAL IMPROVEMENT OF HUMAN REASON

VI. In the matter of knowledge, there is between the angels of God and the children of men this difference: angels already have full and complete knowledge in the highest degree that can be imparted unto them; men, if we view them in their spring, are at the first without understanding or knowledge at all [Isaiah vii.16]. Nevertheless from this utter vacuity they grow by degrees, till they come at length to be even as the angels themselves are. That which agreeth to the one now, the other shall attain unto in the end; they are not so far disjoined and severed, but that they come at length to meet. The soul of man being therefore at the first as a book, wherein nothing is and yet all things may be imprinted; we are to search by what steps and degrees it riseth unto perfection of knowledge.

[2] Unto that which hath been already set down concerning natural agents this we must add, that albeit therein we have comprised as well creatures living as void of life, if they be in degree of nature beneath men; nevertheless a difference we must observe between those natural agents that work altogether unwittingly, and those which have though weak yet some understanding what they do, as fishes, fowls, and beasts have. Beasts are in sensible capacity as ripe even as men themselves, perhaps more ripe. For as stones, though in dignity of nature inferior unto plants, yet exceed them in firmness of strength or durability of being; and plants, though beneath the excellency of creatures

endued with sense, yet exceed them in the faculty of vegetation and of fertility: so beasts, though otherwise behind men, may notwithstanding in actions of sense and fancy go beyond them; because the endeavours of nature, when it hath a higher perfection to seek, are in lower the more remiss, not esteeming thereof so much as those things do, which have no better proposed unto them.

[3] The soul of man therefore being capable of a more divine perfection, hath (besides the faculties of growing unto sensible knowledge which is common unto us with beasts) a further ability, whereof in them there is no show at all, the ability of reaching higher than unto sensible things. Till we grow to some ripeness of years, the soul of man doth only store itself with conceits of things inferior and more open quality, which afterwards do serve as instruments unto that which is greater; in the meanwhile above the reach of meaner creatures it ascendeth not. When once it comprehendeth any thing above this, as the differences of time, affirmations, negations, and contradictions in speech, we then count it to have some use of natural reason. Whereunto if afterwards there might be added the right helps of true art and learning (which helps, I must plainly confess, this age of the world, carrying the name of a learned age, doth neither much know nor greatly regard), there would undoubtedly be almost as great difference in maturity of judgment between men therewith inured, and that which now men are, as between men that are now and innocents....

[5] Education and instruction are the means, the one by use, the other by precept, to make our natural faculty of reason both the better and the sooner able to judge rightly between truth and error, good and evil. But at what time a man may be said to have attained so far forth the use of reason, as sufficeth to make him capable of those Laws, whereby he is then bound to guide his actions; this is a great deal more easy for common sense to discern, than for any man by skill and learning to determine; even as it is not in philosophers, who best know the nature both of fire and of gold, to teach what degree of the one will serve to purify the other, so well as the artisan, who doth this by fire, discerneth

by sense when the fire hath that degree of heat which sufficeth
for his purpose.   (I.vi.1-3, 5)

11   WILL, APPETITE AND REASON

VII. By reason man attaineth unto the knowledge of things
that are and are not sensible. It resteth therefore that we search
how man attaineth unto the knowledge of such things unsensible
as are to be known that they may be done. Seeing then that
nothing can move unless there be some end, the desire whereof
provoketh unto motion; how should that divine power of the
soul, that "spirit of our mind" [Eph. iv.23] as the apostle termeth
it, ever stir itself unto action, unless it have also the like spur?
The end for which we are moved to work, is sometimes the goodness which we conceive of the very working itself, without any
further respect at all; and the cause that procureth action is the
mere desire of action, no other good besides being thereby
intended. Of certain turbulent wits it is said, "Illis quieta movere
magna merces videbatur"[1] they thought the very disturbance of
things established an hire sufficient to set them on work. Sometimes that which we do is referred to a further end, without the
desire whereof we would leave the same undone; as in their
actions that gave alms to purchase thereby the praise of men
[Matthew vi.2].

[2] Man in perfection of nature being made according to the
likeness of his Maker resembleth him also in the manner of working: so that whatsoever we work as men, the same we do wittingly
work and freely; neither are we according to the manner of natural
agents any way so tied, but that it is in our power to leave the
things we do undone. The good which either is gotten by doing,
or which consisteth in the very doing itself, causeth not action,
unless apprehending it as good we so like and desire it: that we
do unto any such end, the same we choose and prefer before the

1   Sallust, *Catiline* 22.

leaving of it undone. Choice there is not, unless the thing which
we take be so in our power that we might have refused and left
it. If fire consume the stubble, it chooseth not so to do, because
the nature thereof is such that it can do no other. To choose is
to will one thing before another. And to will is to bend our souls
to the having or doing of that which they see to be good. Goodness is seen with the eye of the understanding. And the light of
that eye, is reason. So that two principal fountains there are of
human action, Knowledge and Will; which Will, in things tending
towards any end, is termed Choice. Concerning Knowledge, "Behold, (saith Moses), I have set before you this day good and evil,
life and death" [Deut. xxx.19]. Concerning Will, he addeth
immediately, "Choose life"; that is to say, the things that tend
unto life, them choose.

[3] But of one thing we must have special care, as being a matter
of no small moment; and that is, how the Will, properly and
strictly taken, as it is of things which are referred unto the end
that man desireth, differeth greatly from that inferior natural
desire which we call Appetite. The object of Appetite is whatsoever sensible good may be wished for; the object of Will is that
good which Reason doth lead us to seek. Affections, as joy, and
grief, and fear, and anger, with such like, being as it were the
sundry fashions and forms of Appetite, can neither rise at the
conceit of a thing indifferent, nor yet choose but rise at the sight
of some things. Wherefore it is not altogether in our power,
whether we will be stirred with affections or no: whereas actions
which issue from the disposition of the Will are in the power
thereof to be performed or stayed. Finally, Appetite is the Will's
solicitor, and the Will is Appetite's controller; what we covet
according to the one by the other we often reject; neither is any
other desire termed properly Will, but that where Reason and
Understanding, or the show of Reason, prescribeth the thing
desired.

It may be therefore a question, whether those operations of
men are to be counted voluntary, wherein that good which is
sensible provoketh Appetite, and Appetite causeth action,
Reason being never called to counsel; as when we eat or drink,

and betake ourselves unto rest, and such like. The truth is, that such actions in men having attained to the use of Reason are voluntary. For as the authority of higher powers hath force even in those things, which are done without their privity, and are of so mean reckoning that to acquaint them therewith it needeth , not; in like sort, voluntarily we are said to do that also, which the Will if it listed might hinder from being done, although about the doing thereof we do not expressly use our reason or understanding, and so immediately apply our wills thereunto. In cases therefore of such facility, the Will doth yield her assent as it were with a kind of silence, by not dissenting; in which respect her force is not so apparent as in express mandates or prohibitions, especially upon advice and consultation going before.

[4] Where understanding therefore needeth, in those things Reason is the director of man's Will by discovering in action what is good. For the Laws of well-doing are the dictates of right Reason. Children, which are not as yet come unto those years whereat they may have; again, innocents, which are excluded by natural defect from ever having; thirdly, madmen, which for the present cannot possibly have the use of right Reason to guide themselves, have for their guide the Reason that guideth other men, which are tutors over them to seek and to procure their good for them. In the rest there is that light of Reason, whereby good may be known from evil, and which discovering the same rightly is termed right.

[5] The Will notwithstanding doth not incline to have or do that which Reason teacheth to be good, unless the same do also teach it to be possible. For albeit the Appetite, being more general, may wish any thing which seemeth good, be it never so impossible; yet for such things the reasonable Will of man doth never seek. Let Reason teach impossibility in any thing, and the Will of man doth let it go; a thing impossible it doth not effect, the impossibility thereof being manifest.

[6] There is in the Will of man naturally that freedom, whereby it is apt to take or refuse any particular object whatsoever being presented unto it. Whereupon it followeth, that there is no particular object so good, but it may have the shew of some difficulty

or unpleasant quality annexed to it, in respect thereof the Will may shrink and decline it; contrariwise (for so things are blended) there is no particular evil which hath not some appearance of goodness whereby to insinuate itself. For evil as evil cannot be desired: if that be desired which is evil, the cause is the goodness which is or seemeth to be joined with it. Goodness doth not move by being, but by being apparent; and therefore many things are neglected which are most precious, only because the value of them lieth hid. Sensible Goodness is most apparent, near, and present; which causeth the Appetite to be therewith strongly provoked. Now pursuit and refusal in the Will do follow, the one the affirmation the other the negation of goodness, which the understanding apprehendeth, grounding itself upon sense, unless some higher Reason do chance to teach the contrary. And if Reason have taught it rightly to be good, yet not so apparently that the mind receiveth it with utter impossibility of being otherwise, still there is place left for the Will to take or leave. Whereas therefore amongst so many things as are to be done, there are so few, the goodness whereof Reason in such sort doth or easily can discover, we are not to marvel at the choice of evil even then when the contrary is probably known. Hereby it cometh to pass that custom inuring the mind by long practice, and so leaving there a sensible impression, prevaileth more than reasonable persuasion what way soever. Reason therefore may rightly discern the thing which is good, and yet the Will of man not incline itself thereunto, as oft as the prejudice of sensible experience doth oversway.

[7] Nor let any man think that this doth make any thing for the just excuse of iniquity. For there was never sin committed, wherein a less good was not preferred before a greater, and that wilfully; which cannot be done without the singular disgrace of Nature, and the utter disturbance of that divine order, whereby the preeminence of chiefest acceptation is by the best things worthily challenged. There is not that good which concerneth us, but it hath evidence enough for itself, if Reason were diligent to search it out. Through neglect thereof, abused we are with the show of that which is not; sometimes the subtilty of Satan inveigling

us as it did Eve [2 Cor. xi.3], sometimes the hastiness of our Wills preventing the more considerate advice of sound Reason, as in the Apostles, when they no sooner saw what they liked not, but they forthwith were desirous of fire from heaven [Luke ix.54]; sometimes the very custom of evil making the heart obdurate against whatsoever instructions to the contrary, as in them over whom our Saviour spake weeping, "O Jerusalem, how often, and thou wouldest not!" [Matthew xxiii.37]. Still therefore that wherewith we stand blameable, and can no way excuse it, is, In doing evil, we prefer a less good before a greater, the greatness whereof is by reason investigable and may be known. The search of knowledge is a thing painful; and the painfulness of knowledge is that which maketh the Will so hardly inclinable thereunto. The root hereof, divine malediction; whereby the instruments being weakened wherewithal the soul (especially in reasoning) doth work, it preferreth rest in ignorance before wearisome labour to know. For a spur of diligence therefore we have a natural thirst after knowledge ingrafted in us. But by reason of that original weakness in the instruments, without which the understanding part is not able in this world by discourse to work, the very conceit of painfulness is as a bridle to stay us. For which cause the Apostle, who knew right well that the weariness of the flesh is an heavy clog to the Will, striketh mightily upon this key, "Awake thou that sleepest; Cast off all which presseth down; Watch; Labour; Strive to go forward, and to grow in knowledge" [Ephes. v.14; Hebrews xii.1, 12; 1 Cor. xvi.14; Proverbs ii.4; Luke xiii.24].

(I.vii)

12　IDENTIFYING VIRTUE

VIII. Wherefore to return to our former intent of discovering the natural way, whereby rules have been found out concerning that goodness wherewith the Will of man ought to be moved in human actions; as every thing naturally and necessarily doth desire the utmost good and greatest perfection whereof Nature hath made it capable, even so man. Our felicity therefore being the object and accomplishment of our desire, we cannot choose but wish and covet it. All particular things which are subject unto action, the Will doth so far forth incline unto, as Reason judgeth them the better for us, and consequently the more available to our bliss. If Reason err, we fall into evil, and are so far forth deprived of the general perfection we seek. Seeing therefore that for the framing of men's actions the knowledge of good from evil is necessary, it only resteth that we search how this may be had. Neither must we suppose that there needeth one rule to know the good and another the evil by. For he that knoweth what is straight doth even thereby discern what is crooked, because the absence of straightness in bodies capable thereof is crookedness. Goodness in actions is like unto straightness; wherefore that which is done well we term *right*. For as the straight way is most acceptable to him that travelleth, because by it he cometh soonest to his journey's end; so in action, that which doth lie the evenest between us and the end we desire must needs be the fittest for our use. Besides which fitness for use, there is also in rectitude, beauty; as contrariwise in obliquity, deformity. And that which is good in the actions of men, doth not only delight as profitable, but as amiable also. In which consideration the Grecians most divinely have given to the active perfection of men a name expressing both beauty and goodness, because goodness in ordinary speech is for the most part applied only to that which is beneficial. But we in the name of goodness do here imply both.

[2] And of discerning goodness there are but these two ways; the one the knowledge of the causes whereby it is made such; the other the observation of those signs and tokens, which being annexed always unto goodness, argue that where they are found, there also goodness is, although we know not the cause by force whereof it is there. The former of these is the most sure and infallible way, but so hard that all shun it, and had rather walk as men do in the dark by haphazard, than tread so long and intricate mazes for knowledge' sake. As therefore physicians are many times forced to leave such methods of curing as themselves know to be the fittest, and being overruled by their patients'

impatiency are fain to try the best they can, in taking that way of cure which the cured will yield unto; in like sort, considering how the case doth stand with this present age full of tongue and weak of brain, behold we yield to the stream thereof; into the causes of goodness we will not make any curious or deep inquiry; to touch them now and then it shall be sufficient, when they are so near at hand that easily they may be conceived without any far-removed discourse: that way we are contented to prove, which being the worse in itself, is notwithstanding now by reason of common imbecility the fitter and likelier to be brooked.

[3] Signs and tokens to know good by are of sundry kinds; some more certain and some less. The most certain token of evident goodness is, if the general persuasion of all men do so account it. And therefore a common received error is never utterly overthrown, till such time as we go from signs unto causes, and shew some manifest root or fountain thereof common unto all, whereby it may clearly appear how it hath come to pass that so many have been overseen. In which case surmises and slight probabilities will not serve, because the universal consent of men is the perfectest and strongest in this kind, which comprehendeth only the signs and tokens of goodness. Things casual do vary, and that which a man doth but chance to think well of cannot still have the like hap. Wherefore although we know not the cause, yet thus much we may know; that some necessary cause there is, whensoever the judgments of all men generally or for the most part run one and the same way, especially in matters of natural discourse. For of things necessarily and naturally done there is no more affirmed but this, "They keep either always or for the most part one tenure".[1] The general and perpetual voice of men is as the sentence of God himself. For that which all men have at all times learned, Nature herself must needs have taught; and God being the author of Nature, her voice is but his instrument. By her from Him we receive whatsoever in such sort we learn. Infinite duties there are, the goodness whereof is by this rule sufficiently manifested, although we had no other warrant

1   Aristotle, *Rhetoric*, I.10.

besides to approve them. The Apostle St. Paul having speech concerning the heathen saith of them, "They are a law unto themselves" [Romans ii.14]. His meaning is, that by force of the light of Reason, wherewith God illuminateth every one which cometh into the world, men being enabled to know truth from falsehood, and good from evil, do thereby learn in many things what the will of God is; which will himself not revealing by any extraordinary means unto them, but they by natural discourse attaining the knowledge thereof, seem the makers of those Laws which indeed are his, and they but only the finders of them out.

[4] A law therefore generally taken, is a directive rule unto goodness of operation. The rule of divine operations outward, is the definitive appointment of God's own wisdom set down within himself. The rule of natural agents that work by simple necessity, is the determination of the wisdom of God, known to God himself the principal director of them, but not unto them that are directed to execute the same. The rule of natural agents which work after a sort of their own accord, as the beasts do, is the judgment of common sense or fancy concerning the sensible goodness of those objects wherewith they are moved. The rule of ghostly or immaterial natures, as spirits and angels, is their intuitive intellectual judgment concerning the amiable beauty and high goodness of that object, which with unspeakable joy and delight doth set them on work. The rule of voluntary agents on earth is the sentence that Reason giveth concerning the goodness of those things which they are to do. And the sentences which Reason giveth are some more some less general, before it come to define in particular actions what is good.

[5] The main principles of Reason are in themselves apparent. For to make nothing evident of itself unto man's understanding were to take away all possibility of knowing any thing. And herein that of Theophrastus is true, "They that seek a reason of all things do utterly overthrow Reason". In every kind of knowledge some such grounds there are, as that being proposed the mind doth presently embrace them as free from all possibility of error, clear and manifest without proof. In which kind axioms or principles more general are such as this, "that the greater good

is to be chosen before the less". If therefore it should be demanded what reason there is, why the Will of Man, which doth necessarily shun harm and covet whatsoever is pleasant and sweet, should be commanded to count the pleasures of sin gall, and notwithstanding the bitter accidents wherewith virtuous actions are compassed, yet still to rejoice and delight in them: surely this could never stand with Reason, but that wisdom thus prescribing groundeth her laws upon an infallible rule of comparison; which is, "That small difficulties, when exceeding great good is sure to ensue, and on the other side momentary benefits, when the hurt which they draw after them is unspeakable, are not at all to be respected". This rule is the ground whereupon the wisdom of the Apostle buildeth a law, enjoining patience unto himself; "The present lightness of our affliction worketh unto us even with abundance upon abundance an eternal weight of glory; while we look not on the things which are seen, but on the things which are not seen: for the things which are seen are temporal, but the things which are not seen are eternal" [2 Cor. iv.17]: therefore Christianity to be embraced, whatsoever calamities in those times it was accompanied withal. Upon the same ground our Saviour proveth the law most reasonable, that doth forbid those crimes which men for gain's sake fall into. "For a man to win the world if it be with the loss of his soul, what benefit or good is it?" [Matthew xvi.26]. Axioms less general, yet so manifest that they need no further proof, are such as these, "God to be worshipped"; "parents to be honoured"; "others to be used by us as we ourselves would by them". Such things, as soon as they are alleged, all men acknowledge to be good; they require no proof or further discourse to be assured of their goodness.

Notwithstanding whatsoever such principle there is, it was at the first found out by discourse, and drawn from out of the very bowels of heaven and earth. For we are to note, that things in the world are to us discernible, not only so far forth as serveth for our vital preservation, but further also in a twofold higher respect. For first if all other uses were utterly taken away, yet the mind of man being by nature speculative and delighted with contemplation in itself, they were to be known even for mere knowledge and understanding's sake. Yea further besides this, the knowledge of every the least thing in the whole world hath in it a second peculiar benefit unto us, inasmuch as it serveth to minister rules, canons, and laws, for men to direct those actions by, which we properly term human. This did the very heathens themselves obscurely insinuate, by making *Themis*, which we call *Jus*, or Right, to be the daughter of heaven and earth.

[6] We know things either as they are in themselves, or as they are in mutual relation one to another. The knowledge of that which man is in reference unto himself, and other things in relation unto man, I may justly term the mother of all those principles, which are as it were edicts, statutes, and decrees, in that Law of Nature, whereby human actions are framed. First therefore having observed that the best things, where they are not hindered, do still produce the best operations, (for which cause, where many things are to concur unto one effect, the best is in all congruity of reason to guide the residue, that it prevailing most, the work principally done by it may have the greatest perfection:) when hereupon we come to observe in ourselves, of what excellency our souls are in comparison of our bodies, and the diviner part in relation unto the baser of our souls; seeing that all these concur in producing human actions, it cannot be well unless the chiefest do command and direct the rest. The soul then ought to conduct the body, and the spirit of our minds the soul. This is therefore the first Law, whereby the highest power of the mind requireth general obedience at the hands of all the rest concurring with it unto action.

[7] Touching the several grand mandates, which being imposed by the understanding faculty of the mind must be obeyed by the Will of Man, they are by the same method found out, whether they import our duty towards God or towards man.

Touching the one, I may not here stand to open, by what degrees of discourse the minds even of mere natural men have attained to know, not only that there is a God, but also what power, force, wisdom, and other properties that God hath, and how all things depend on him. This being therefore presupposed, from that known relation which God hath unto us as unto children, and unto all good things as unto effects whereof himself is the principal cause, these axioms and laws natural concerning our duty have arisen, "that in all things we go about his aid is by prayer to be craved":[1] "that he cannot have sufficient honour done unto him, but the utmost of that we can do to honour him we must"[2] which is in effect the same that we read, "Thou shalt love the Lord thy God with all thy heart, with all thy soul, and with all thy mind" [Deut. vi.5]; which Law our Saviour doth term "The first and the great commandment" [Matthew xxii.38].

Touching the next, which as our Saviour addeth is "like unto this", (he meaneth in amplitude and largeness, inasmuch as it is the root out of which all Laws of duty to men-ward have grown, as out of the former all offices of religion towards God), the like natural inducement hath brought men to know that it is their duty no less to love others than themselves. For seeing those things which are equal must needs all have one measure; if I cannot but wish to receive all good, even as much at every man's hand as any man can wish unto his own soul, how should I look to have any part of my desire herein satisfied, unless myself be careful to satisfy the like desire which is undoubtedly in other men, we all being of one and the same nature? To have any thing offered them repugnant to this desire must needs in all respects grieve them as much as me: so that if I do harm I must look to suffer; there being no reason that others should shew greater measure of love to me than they have by me shewed unto them. My desire therefore to be loved of my equals in nature as much as possible may be, imposeth upon me a natural duty of bearing to them-ward fully the like affection. From which relation of equality between ourselves and them that are as ourselves, what several rules and canons natural Reason hath drawn for direction of life no man is ignorant; as namely, "That because we would take no harm, we must therefore do none"; "That sith we would not be in any thing extremely dealt with, we must ourselves avoid all extremity in our dealings"; "That from all violence and wrong

1   Plato, *Timaeus*, III.27.
2   Aristotle, *Ethics*, III.

we are utterly to abstain"; with such like; which further to wade
in would be tedious, and to our present purpose not altogether
so necessary, seeing that on these two general heads already
mentioned all other specialities are dependent [Matthew xxii.40].

[8] Wherefore the natural measure whereby to judge our doings,
is the sentence of Reason, determining and setting down what
is good to be done. Which sentence is either mandatory, shewing
what must be done; or else permissive, declaring only what may
be done; or thirdly admonitory, opening what is the most convenient for us to do. The first taketh place, where the comparison
doth stand altogether between doing and not doing of one thing
which in itself is absolutely good or evil; as it had been for Joseph
to yield or not to yield to the impotent desire of his lewd mistress
[Genesis xxxix.9], the one evil the other good simply. The second
is, when of divers things evil, all being not evitable, we are permitted to take one; which one saving only in case of so great urgency
were not otherwise to be taken; as in the matter of divorce amongst
the Jews [Mark x.4]. The last, when of divers things good, one
is principal and most eminent; as in their act who sold their possessions and laid the price at the Apostles' feet [Acts iv.37; v.4];
which possessions they might have retained unto themselves
without sin: again, in the Apostle St. Paul's own choice to maintain himself by his own labour [2 Thess. iii.8]; whereas in living
by the Church's maintenance, as others did, there had been no
offence committed. In Goodness therefore there is a latitude or
extent, whereby it cometh to pass that even of good actions some
are better than other some: whereas otherwise one man could
not excel another, but all should be either absolutely good, as
hitting jump that indivisible point or centre wherein goodness
consisteth; or else missing it they should be excluded out of the
number of well-doers. Degrees of well-doing there could be none,
except perhaps in the seldomness and oftenness of doing well.
But the nature of Goodness being thus ample, a law is properly
that which Reason in such sort defineth to be good that it must
be done. And the Law of Reason or human Nature is that which
men by discourse of natural Reason have rightly found out themselves to be all for ever bound unto in their actions.

[9] Laws of Reason have these marks to be known by. Such as
keep them resemble most lively in their voluntary actions that
very manner of working which Nature herself doth necessarily
observe in the course of the whole world. The works of Nature
are all behoveful, beautiful, without superfluity or defect; even
so theirs, if they be framed according to that which the Law of
Reason teacheth. Secondly, those Laws are investigable by
Reason, without the help of Revelation supernatural and divine.
Finally, in such sort they are investigable, that the knowledge of
them is general, the world hath always been acquainted with
them; according to that which one in Sophocles observeth concerning a branch of this Law, "It is no child of to-day's or yester-
day's birth, but hath been no man knoweth how long sithence".[1]
It is not agreed upon by one, or two, or few, but by all. Which
we may not so understand, as if every particular man in the
whole world did know and confess whatsoever the Law of Reason
doth contain; but this Law is such that being proposed no man
can reject it as unreasonable and unjust. Again, there is nothing
in it but any man (having natural perfection of wit and ripeness
of judgment) may by labour and travail find out. And to conclude,
the general principles thereof are such, as it is not easy to find
men ignorant of them, Law rational therefore, which men commonly use to call the Law of Nature, meaning thereby the Law
which human Nature knoweth itself in reason universally bound
unto, which also for that cause may be termed most fitly the Law
of Reason; this Law, I say, comprehendeth all those things which
men by the light of their natural understanding evidently know,
or at leastwise may know, to be beseeming or unbeseeming, virtuous or vicious, good or evil for them to do.

[10] Now although it be true, which some have said, that "whatsoever is done amiss, the Law of Nature and Reason thereby is
transgressed"[2] because even those offences which are by their
special qualities breaches of supernatural laws, do also, for that
they are generally evil, violate in general that principle of Reason,

1   Sophocles, *Antigone*, 456.
2   Augustine, *City of God*, XII.1.

which willeth universally to fly from evil: yet do we not therefore
so far extend the Law of Reason, as to contain in it all manner
laws whereunto reasonable creatures are bound, but (as hath
been shewed) we restrain it to those only duties, which all men
by force of natural wit either do or might understand to be such
duties as concern all men. "Certain half-waking men there are"
(as Saint Augustine noteth) "who neither altogether asleep in
folly, nor yet throughly awake in the light of true understanding,
have thought that there is not at all any thing just and righteous
in itself; but look, wherewith nations are inured, the same they
take to be right and just. Whereupon their conclusion is, that
seeing each sort of people hath a different kind of right from
other, and that which is right of its own nature must be every-
where one and the same, therefore in itself there is nothing right.
These good folk," saith he, ("that I may not trouble their wits
with rehearsal of too many things), have not looked so far into
the world as to perceive that, 'Do as thou wouldest be done unto',
is a sentence which all nations under heaven are agreed upon.
Refer this sentence to the love of God, and it extinguisheth all
heinous crimes; refer it to the love of thy neighbour, and all grievous wrongs it banisheth out of the world".[1] Wherefore as touching the Law of Reason, this was (it seemeth) Saint Augustine's
judgment: namely, that there are in it some things which stand
as principles universally agreed upon; and that out of those principles, which are in themselves evident, the greatest moral duties
we owe towards God or man may without any great difficulty
be concluded.

[11] If then it be here demanded, by what means it should
come to pass (the greatest part of the Law moral being so easy
for all men to know) that so many thousands of men notwithstanding have been ignorant even of principal moral duties, not
imagining the breach of them to be sin: I deny not but lewd and
wicked custom, beginning perhaps at the first amongst few, afterwards spreading into greater multitudes, and so continuing from
time to time, may be of force even in plain things to smother the

1   Augustine, *Christian Doctrine*, III.13.

light of natural understanding; because men will not bend their wits to examine whether things wherewith they have been accustomed be good or evil. For example's sake, that grosser kind of heathenish idolatry, whereby they worshipped the very works of their own hands, was an absurdity to reason so palpable, that the Prophet David comparing idols and idolators together maketh almost no odds between them, but the one in a manner as much without wit and sense as the other; "They that make them are like unto them, and so are all that trust in them" [Psalm cxxxv. 18]. That wherein an idolator doth seem so absurd and foolish is by the Wise Man thus exprest, "He is not ashamed to speak unto that which hath no life, he calleth on him that is weak for health, he prayeth for life unto him which is dead, of him which hath no experience he requireth help, for his journey he sueth to him which is not able to go, for gain and work and success in his affairs he seeketh furtherance of him that hath no manner of power" [Wisdom xiii. 17]. The cause of which senseless stupidity is afterwards imputed to custom. "When a father mourned grievously for his son that was taken away suddenly, he made an image for him that was once dead, whom now he worshippeth as a god, ordaining to his servants ceremonies and sacrifices. Thus by process of time this wicked custom prevailed, and was kept as a law" [Wisdom xiv. 15-16]; the authority of rulers, the ambition of craftsmen, and such like means thrusting forward the ignorant, and increasing their superstition.

Unto this which the Wise Man hath spoken somewhat besides may be added. For whatsoever we have hitherto taught, or shall hereafter, concerning the force of man's natural understanding, this we always desire withal to be understood; that there is no kind of faculty or power in man or any other creature, which can rightly perform the functions allotted to it, without perpetual aid and concurrence of that Supreme Cause of all things. The benefit whereof as oft as we cause God in his justice to withdraw, there can no other thing follow than that which the Apostle noteth, even men endued with the light of reason to walk notwithstanding "in the vanity of their mind, having their cogitations darkened, and being strangers from the life of God through the ignorance which is in them, because of the hardness of their hearts" [Ephes. iv.17-18]. And this cause is mentioned by the prophet Esay, speaking of the ignorance of idolators, who see not how the manifest Law of Reason condemneth their gross iniquity and sin. "They have not in them", saith he, "so much wit as to think, 'Shall I bow to the stock of a tree?' All knowledge and understanding is taken from them; for God hath shut their eyes that they cannot see" [Isaiah xliv.18-19].

That which we say in this case of idolatry serveth for all other things, wherein the like kind of general blindness hath prevailed against the manifest Laws of Reason. Within the compass of which laws we do not only comprehend whatsoever may be easily known to belong to the duty of all men, but even whatsoever may possibly be known to be of that quality, so that the same be by *necessary* consequence deduced out of clear and manifest principles. For if once we descend unto probable collections what is convenient for men, we are then in the territory where free and arbitrary determinations, the territory where Human Laws take place; which laws are after to be considered.   (I.viii)

13   VALUE IN OBSERVING LAW

IX. Now the due observation of this Law which Reason teacheth us cannot but be effectual unto their great good that observe the same. For we see the whole world and each part thereof so compacted, that as long as each thing performeth only that work which is natural unto it, it thereby preserveth both other things and also itself. Contrariwise, let any principal thing, as the sun, the moon, any one of the heavens or elements, but once cease or fail, or swerve, and who doth not easily conceive that the sequel thereof would be ruin both to itself and whatsoever dependeth on it? And is it possible, that Man being not only the noblest creature in the world, but even a very world in himself, his transgressing the Law of his Nature should draw no manner of harm after it? Yes, "tribulation and anguish unto every soul that doeth

evil" [Romans ii.9]. Good doth follow unto all things by observing
the course of their nature, and on the contrary side evil by not
observing it; but not unto natural agents that good which we call
Reward, not that evil which we properly term Punishment. The
reason whereof is, because amongst creatures in this world, only
Man's observation of the Law of his Nature is Righteousness,
only Man's transgression Sin. And the reason of this is the difference in his manner of observing or transgressing the Law of his
Nature. He doth not otherwise than voluntarily the one or the
other. What we do against our wills, or constrainedly, we are
not properly said to do it, because the motive cause of doing it
is not in ourselves, but carrieth us, as if the wind should drive a
feather in the air, we no whit furthering that whereby we are
driven. In such cases therefore the evil which is done moveth
compassion; men are pitied for it, as being rather miserable in
such respect than culpable. Some things are likewise done by
man, though not through outward force and impulsion, though
not against, yet without their wills; as in alienation of mind, or
any the like inevitable utter absence of wit and judgment. For
which cause, no man did ever think the hurtful actions of furious
men and innocents to be punishable. Again, some things we do
neither against nor without, and yet not simply and merely with
our wills, but with our wills in such sort moved, that albeit there
be no impossibility but that we might, nevertheless we are not
so easily able to do otherwise. In this consideration one evil deed
is made more pardonable than another. Finally, that which we
do being evil, is notwithstanding by so much more pardonable,
by how much the exigence of so doing or the difficulty of doing
otherwise is greater; unless this necessity or difficulty have originally risen from ourselves. It is no excuse therefore unto him,
who being drunk committeth incest, and allegeth that his wits
were not his own; inasmuch as himself might have chosen
whether his wits should by that mean have been taken from him.
Now rewards and punishments do always presuppose something willingly done well or ill; without which respect though
we may sometimes receive good or harm, yet then the one is
only a benefit and not a reward, the other simply an hurt not a

punishment. From the sundry dispositions of man's Will, which is the root of all his actions, there groweth variety in the sequel of rewards and punishments, which are by these and the like rules measured: "Take away the will, and all acts are equal: That which we do not, and would do, is commonly accepted as done".[1] By these and the like rules men's actions are determined of and judged, whether they be in their own nature rewardable or punishable.

[2] Rewards and punishments are not received, but at the hands of such as being above us have power to examine and judge our deeds. How men come to have this authority one over another in external actions, we shall more diligently examine in that which followeth. But for this present, so much all do acknowledge, that sith every man's heart and conscience doth in good or evil, even secretly committed and known to none but itself, either like or disallow itself, and accordingly either rejoice, very nature exulting (as it were) in certain hope of reward, or else grieve (as it were) in a sense of future punishment; neither of which can in this case be looked for from any other, saving only from Him who discerneth and judgeth the very secrets of all hearts: therefore He is the only rewarder and revenger of all such actions; although not of such actions only, but of all whereby the Law of Nature is broken whereof Himself is author. For which cause, the Roman Laws, called The Laws of the Twelve Tables, requiring offices of inward affection which the eye of man cannot reach unto, threaten the neglecters of them with none but divine punishment.[2]   (I.ix)

14   LAW, SOCIETY AND GOVERNMENT

X. That which hitherto we have set down is (I hope) sufficient to shew their brutishness, which imagine that religion and virtue

1   Justinian, *Codex*, 968, 732.
2   Cicero, *De Legibus*, II.8.

are only as men will account of them; that we might make as much account, if we would, of the contrary, without any harm unto ourselves, and that in nature they are as indifferent one as the other. We see then how nature itself teacheth laws and statutes to live by. The laws which have been hitherto mentioned do bind men absolutely even as they are men, although they have never any settled fellowship, never any solemn agreement amongst themselves what to do or not to do.[1] But forasmuch as we are not by ourselves sufficient to furnish ourselves with competent store of things needful for such a life as our nature doth desire, a life fit for the dignity of man; therefore to supply those defects and imperfections which are in us living single and solely by ourselves, we are naturally induced to seek communion and fellowship with others. This was the cause of men's uniting themselves at the first in politic Societies, which societies could not be without Government, nor Government without a distinct kind of Law from that which hath been already declared. Two foundations there are which bear up public societies; the one, a natural inclination, whereby all men desire sociable life and fellowship; the other, an order expressly or secretly agreed upon touching the manner of their union in living together. The latter is that which we call the Law of a Commonweal, the very soul of a politic body, the parts whereof are by law animated, held together, and set on work in such actions, as the common good requireth. Laws politic, ordained for external order and regiment amongst men, are never framed as they should be, unless presuming the will of man to be inwardly obstinate, rebellious, and averse from all obedience unto the sacred laws of his nature; in a word, unless presuming man to be in regard of his depraved mind little better than a wild beast, they do accordingly provide notwithstanding so to frame his outward actions, that they be no hindrance unto the common good for which societies are instituted: unless they do this, they are not perfect. It resteth therefore that we consider how nature findeth out such laws of government as serve to direct even nature depraved to a right end.

1 Aristotle, *Poetics*, I.13.

[2] All men desire to lead in this world a happy life. That life is led most happily, wherein all virtue is exercised without impediment or let. The Apostle, in exhorting men to contentment although they have in this world no more than very bare food and raiment, giveth us thereby to understand that those are even the lowest of things necessary; that if we should be stripped of all those things without which we might possibly be, yet these must be left; that destitution in these is such an impediment, as till it be removed suffereth not the mind of man to admit any other care [1 Tim. vi.8]. For this cause, first God assigned Adam maintenance of life, and then appointed him a law to observe [Genesis i.29; ii.17]. For this cause, after men began to grow to a number, the first thing we read they gave themselves unto was the tilling of the earth and the feeding of cattle. Having by this mean whereon to live, the principal actions of their life afterward are noted by the exercise of their religion [Genesis iv.2, 26]. True it is, that the kingdom of God must be the first thing in our purposes and desires [Matthew vi.33]. But inasmuch as righteous life presupposeth life; inasmuch as to live virtuously it is impossible except we live; therefore the first impediment, which naturally we endeavour to remove, is penury and want of things without which we cannot live. Unto life many implements are necessary; moe, if we seek (as all men naturally do) such a life as hath in it joy, comfort, delight, and pleasure. To this end we see how quickly sundry arts mechanical were found out, in the very prime of the world [Genesis iv.20-22]. As things of greatest necessity are always first provided for, so things of greatest dignity are most accounted of by all such as judge rightly. Although therefore riches be a thing which every man wisheth, yet no man of judgment can esteem it better to be rich, than wise, virtuous, and religious. If we be both or either of these, it is not because we are so born. For into the world we come as empty of the one as of the other, as naked in mind as we are in body. Both which necessities of man had at the first no other helps and supplies than only domestical; such as that which the Prophet implieth, saying, "Can a mother forget her child?" [Isaiah xlix.15] such as that which the Apostle mentioneth, saying, "He that careth not

for his own is worse than an infidel" [1 Tim. v.8]; such as that concerning Abraham, "Abraham will command his sons and his household after him, that they keep the way of the Lord" [Genesis xviii.15].

[3] But neither that which we learn of ourselves nor that which others teach us can prevail, where wickedness and malice have taken deep root. If therefore when there was but as yet one only family in the world, no means of instruction human or divine could prevent effusion of blood; how could it be chosen but that when families were multiplied and increased upon earth, after separation each providing for itself, envy, strife, contention and violence must grow amongst them? For hath not Nature furnished man with wit and valour, as it were with armour, which may be used as well unto extreme evil as good? Yea, were they not used by the rest of the world unto evil; unto the contrary only by Seth, Enoch, and those few the rest in that line? [Genesis vi.5;v]. We all make complaint of the iniquity of our times: not unjustly; for the days are evil. But compare them with those times wherein there were no civil societies, with those times wherein there was as yet no manner of public regiment established, with those times wherein there were not above eight persons righteous living upon the face of the earth [2 Peter ii.5]; and we have surely good cause to think that God hath blessed us exceedingly, and hath made us behold most happy days.

[4] To take away all such mutual grievances, injuries, and wrongs, there was no way but only by growing unto composition and agreement amongst themselves, by ordaining some kind of government public, and by yielding themselves subject thereunto; that unto whom they granted authority to rule and govern, by them the peace, tranquillity, and happy estate of the rest might be procured. Men always knew that when force and injury was offered they might be defenders of themselves; they knew that howsoever men may seek their own commodity, yet if this were done with injury unto others it was not to be suffered, but by all men and by all good means to be withstood; finally they knew that no man might in reason take upon him to determine his own right, and according to his own determination proceed in maintenance

thereof, inasmuch as every man is towards himself and them whom he greatly affecteth partial; and therefore that strifes and troubles would be endless, except they gave their common consent all to be ordered by some whom they should agree upon: without which consent there were no reason that one man should take upon him to be lord or judge over another; because, although there be according to the opinion of some very great and judicious men a kind of natural right in the noble, wise, and virtuous, to govern them which are of servile disposition;[1] nevertheless for manifestation of this their right, and men's more peaceable contentment on both sides, the assent of them who are to be governed seemeth necessary.

To fathers within their private families Nature hath given a supreme power; for which cause we see throughout the world even from the foundation thereof, all men have ever been taken as lords and lawful kings in their own houses. Howbeit over a whole grand multitude having no such dependency upon any one, and consisting of so many families as every politic society in the world doth, impossible it is that any should have complete lawful power, but by consent of men, or immediate appointment of God; because not having the natural superiority of fathers, their power must needs be either usurped, and then unlawful; or, if lawful, then either granted or consented unto them over whom they exercise the same, or else given extraordinarily from God, unto whom all the world is subject. It is no improbable opinion therefore which the arch-philosopher was of, that as the chiefest person in every household was always as it were a king, so when numbers of households joined themselves in civil society together, kings were the first kind of governors amongst them.[2] Which is also (as it seemeth) the reason why the name of *Father* continued still in them, who of fathers were made rulers; as also the ancient custom of governors to do as Melchisedec, and being kings to exercise the office of priests, which fathers did at the first, grew perhaps by the same occasion.

1 Aristotle, *Politics*, III and VI.
2 Aristotle, *Politics*, I.2.

Howbeit not this the only kind of regiment that hath been received in the world. The inconveniences of one kind have caused sundry other to be devised. So that in a word all public regiment of what kind soever seemeth evidently to have risen from deliberate advice, consultation, and composition between men, judging it convenient and behoveful; there being no impossibility in nature considered by itself, but that men might have lived without any public regiment. Howbeit, the corruption of our nature being presupposed, we may not deny but that the Law of Nature doth now require of necessity some kind of regiment, so that to bring things unto the first course they were in, and utterly to take away all kind of public government in the world, were apparently to overturn the whole world.

[5] The case of man's nature standing therefore as it doth, some kind of regiment the Law of Nature doth require; yet the kinds thereof being many, Nature tieth not to any one, but leaveth the choice as a thing arbitrary. At the first when some certain kind of regiment was once approved, it may be that nothing was then further thought upon for the manner of governing, but all permitted unto their wisdom and discretion which were to rule;[1] till by experience they found this for all parts very inconvenient, so as the thing which they had devised for a remedy did indeed but increase the sore which it should have cured. They saw that to live by one man's will became the cause of all men's misery. This constrained them to come unto laws, wherein all men might see their duties beforehand, and know the penalties of transgressing them. If things be simply good or evil, and withal universally so acknowledged, there needs no new law to be made for such things. The first kind therefore of things appointed by laws human containeth whatsoever being in itself naturally good or evil, is notwithstanding more secret than that it can be discerned by every man's present conceit, without some deeper discourse and judgment. In which discourse because there is difficulty and possibility many ways to err, unless such things were set down by laws, many would be ignorant of their duties which now are

1   Cicero, *De Officiis*, II.12.

not, and many that know what they should do would nevertheless dissemble it, and to excuse themselves pretend ignorance
and simplicity, which now they cannot.[1]

[6] And because the greatest part of men are such as prefer
their own private good before all things, even that good which
is sensual before whatsoever is most divine; and for that the
labour of doing good, together with the pleasure arising from
the contrary, doth make men for the most part slower to the one
and proner to the other, than that duty prescribed them by law
can prevail sufficiently with them: therefore unto laws that men
do make for the benefit of men it hath seemed always needful
to add rewards, which may more allure unto good than any hardness deterreth from it, and punishments, which may more deter
from evil than any sweetness thereto allureth. Wherein as the
generality is natural, *virtue rewardable and vice punishable*; so the
particular determination of the reward or punishment belongeth
unto them by whom laws are made. Theft is naturally punishable,
but the kind of punishment is positive, and such lawful as men
shall think with discretion convenient by law to appoint.

[7] In laws, that which is natural bindeth universally, that
which is positive not so. To let go those kind of positive laws
which men impose upon themselves, as by vow unto God, con-
tract with men, or such like; somewhat it will make unto our
purpose, a little more fully to consider what things are incident
into the making of the positive laws for the government of them
that live united in public society. Laws do not only teach what
is good, but they enjoin it, they have in them a certain constraining force. And to constrain men unto any thing inconvenient
doth seem unreasonable. Most requisite therefore it is that to
devise laws which all men shall be forced to obey none but wise
men be admitted. Laws are matters of principal consequence;
men of common capacity and but ordinary judgment are not able
(for how should they?) to discern what things are fittest for each
kind and state of regiment. We cannot be ignorant how much
our obedience unto laws dependeth upon this point. Let a man

1 Tertullian, *De Spectaculis*, 1.

though never so justly oppose himself unto them that are disordered in their ways, and what one amongst them commonly doth not stomach at such contradiction, storm at reproof, and hate such as would reform them? Notwithstanding even they which brook it worst that men should tell them of their duties, when they are told the same by a law, think very well and reasonably of it. For why? They presume that the law doth speak with all indifferency; that the law hath no side-respect to their persons; that the law is as it were an oracle proceeded from wisdom and understanding.[1] (I.x.1-7)

15 THE LAW OF NATIONS

[12] Now besides that law which simply concerneth men as men, and that which belongeth unto them as they are men linked with others in some form of politic society, there is a third kind of law which toucheth all such several bodies politic, so far forth as one of them hath public commerce with another. And this third is the Law of Nations. Between men and beasts there is no possibility of sociable communion, because the well-spring of that communion is a natural delight which man hath to transfuse from himself into others, and to receive from others into himself especially those things wherein the excellency of his kind doth most consist. The chiefest instrument of human communion therefore is speech, because thereby we impart mutually one to another the conceits of our reasonable understanding.[2] And for that cause seeing beasts are not hereof capable, forasmuch as with them we can use no such conference, they being in degree, although above other creatures on earth to whom nature hath denied sense, yet lower than to be sociable companions of man to whom nature hath given reason; it is of Adam said that amongst the beasts "he found not for himself any meet companion" [Genesis

1 Aristotle, *Nicomachean Ethics*, X.9.
2 Aristotle, *Politics*, I.2.

ii.20]. Civil society doth more content the nature of man than any private kind of solitary living, because in society this good of mutual participation is so much larger than otherwise. Herewith notwithstanding we are not satisfied, but we covet (if it might be) to have a kind of society and fellowship even with all mankind. Which thing Socrates intending to signify professed himself a citizen, not of this or that commonwealth, but of the world.[1] And an effect of that very natural desire in us (a manifest token that we wish after a sort an universal fellowship with all men) appeareth by the wonderful delight men have, some to visit foreign countries, some to discover nations not heard of in former ages, we all to know the affairs and dealings of other people, yea to be in league of amity with them: and this not only for traffick's sake, or to the end that when many are confederated each may make the other more strong, but for such cause also as moved the Queen of Saba to visit Salomon [1 Kings xi.1; 2 Chr. ix.1; Matthew xii.42; Luke xi.31]; and in a word, because nature doth presume that how many men there are in the world, so many gods as it were there are, or at leastwise such they should be towards men. (I.x.12)

16   THE LAW OF THE CHURCH

[14] Now as there is great cause of communion, and consequently of laws for the maintenance of communion, amongst nations; so amongst nations Christian the like in regard even of Christianity hath been always judged needful.

And in this kind of correspondence amongst nations the force of general councils doth stand. For as one and the same law divine, whereof in the next place we are to speak, is unto all Christian churches a rule for the chiefest things; by means whereof they all in that respect make one church, as having all but "one Lord, one faith, and one baptism" [Eph. iv.5]: so the

---

1   Cicero *Tusculan Disputations*, V.37.

urgent necessity of mutual communion for preservation of our unity in these things, as also for order in some other things convenient to be every where uniformly kept, maketh it requisite that the Church of God here on earth have her laws of spiritual commerce between Christian nations; laws by virtue whereof all churches may enjoy freely the use of those reverend, religious, and sacred consultations, which are termed Councils General. A thing whereof God's own blessed Spirit was the author [Acts xv.28]; a thing practised by the holy Apostles themselves; a thing always afterwards kept and observed throughout the world; a thing never otherwise than most highly esteemed of, till pride, ambition, and tyranny began by factious and vile endeavours to abuse that divine invention unto the furtherance of wicked purposes. But as the just authority of civil courts and parliaments is not therefore to be abolished, because sometime there is cunning used to frame them according to the private intents of men over potent in the commonwealth; so the grievous abuse which hath been of councils should rather cause men to study how so gracious a thing may again be reduced to that first perfection, than in regard of stains and blemishes sithence growing to be held for ever in extreme disgrace.

To speak of this matter as the cause requireth would require very long discourse. All I will presently say is this: whether it be for the finding out of any thing whereunto divine law bindeth us, but yet in such sort that men are not thereof on all sides resolved; or for the setting down of some uniform judgment to stand touching such things, as being neither way matters of necessity, are notwithstanding offensive and scandalous when there is open opposition about them; be it for the ending of strifes, touching matters of Christian belief, wherein the one part may seem to have probable cause of dissenting from the other; or be it concerning matters of polity, order, and regiment in the church; I nothing doubt but that Christian men should much better frame themselves to those heavenly precepts, which our Lord and Saviour with so great instancy gave as concerning peace and unity [John xiv.27], if we did all concur in desire to have the use of ancient councils again renewed, rather than these proceedings continued, which either make all contentions endless, or bring them to one only determination, and that of all other the worst, which is by sword.

[15] It followeth therefore that a new foundation being laid, we now adjoin hereunto that which cometh in the next place to be spoken of; namely, wherefore God hath himself by Scripture made known such laws as serve for direction of men.

(I.x.14-15)

17   MAN'S CHIEF GOOD: THE WAY OF SALVATION

XI. All things, (God only excepted), besides the nature which they have in themselves, receive externally some perfection from other things, as hath been shewed. Insomuch as there is in the whole world no one thing great or small, but either in respect of knowledge or of use it may unto our perfection add somewhat. And whatsoever such perfection there is which our nature may acquire, the same we properly term our Good; our Sovereign Good or Blessedness, that wherein the highest degree of all our perfection consisteth, that which being once attained unto there can rest nothing further to be desired; and therefore with it our souls are fully content and satisfied, in that they have they rejoice, and thirst for no more. Wherefore of good things desired some are such that for themselves we covet them not, but only because they serve as instruments unto that for which we are to seek: of this sort are riches. Another kind there is, which although we desire for itself, as health, and virtue, and knowledge, nevertheless they are not the last mark whereat we aim, but have their further end whereunto they are referred, so as in them we are not satisfied as having attained the utmost we may, but our desires do still proceed. These things are linked and as it were chained one to another; we labour to eat, and we eat to live, and we live to do good, and the good which we do is as seed sown with reference to a future harvest [Gal. vi.8]. But we must come at length to some pause. For, if every thing were to be desired for some other without any stint, there could be no certain end proposed unto our actions, we should go on we know not whither; yea, whatsoever we do were in vain, or rather nothing at all were possible to be done. For as to take away the first efficient of our being were to annihilate utterly our persons, so we cannot remove the last final cause of our working, but we shall cause whatsoever we work to cease. Therefore something there must be desired for itself simply and for no other. That is simply for itself desirable, unto the nature whereof it is opposite and repugnant to be desired with relation unto any other. The ox and the ass desire their food, neither propose they unto themselves any end wherefore; so that of them this is desired for itself; but why? By reason of their imperfection which cannot otherwise desire it; whereas that which is desired simply for itself, the excellency thereof is such as permitteth it not in any sort to be referred to a further end.

[2] Now that which man doth desire with reference to a further end, the same he desireth in such measure as is unto that end convenient; but what he coveteth as good in itself, towards that his desire is ever infinite. So that unless the last good of all, which is desired altogether for itself, be also infinite, we do evil in making it our end; even as they who placed their felicity in wealth or honour or pleasure or any thing here attained; because in desiring any thing as our final perfection which is not so, we do amiss.[1] Nothing may be infinitely desired but that good which indeed is infinite; for the better the more desirable; that therefore most desirable wherein there is infinity of goodness: so that if any thing desirable may be infinite, that must needs be the highest of all things that are desired. No good is infinite but only God; therefore he our felicity and bliss. Moreover, desire tendeth unto union with that it desireth. If then in Him we be blessed, it is by force of participation and conjunction with Him. Again, it is not the possession of any good thing can make them happy which have it, unless they enjoy the thing wherewith they are possessed. Then are we happy therefore when fully we enjoy God, as

1　Aristotle, *Ethics*, X.10.

an object wherein the powers of our souls are satisfied even with everlasting delight; so that although we be men, yet by being unto God united we live as it were the life of God.

[3] Happiness therefore is that estate whereby we attain, so far as possibly may be attained, the full possession of that which simply for itself is to be desired, and containeth in it after an eminent sort the contentation of our desires, the highest degree of all our perfection. Of such perfection capable we are not in this life. For while we are in the world, subject we are unto sundry imperfections, griefs of body, defects of mind; yea the best things we do are painful, and the exercise of them grievous, being continued without intermission; so as in those very actions whereby we are especially perfected in this life we are not able to persist; forced we are with very weariness, and that often, to interrupt them: which tediousness cannot fall into those operations that are in the state of bliss, when our union with God is complete. Complete union with him must be according unto every power and faculty of our minds apt to receive so glorious an object. Capable we are of God both by understanding and will: by understanding, as He is that sovereign Truth which comprehendeth the rich treasures of all wisdom; by will, as He is that sea of Goodness whereof whoso tasteth shall thirst no more. As the will doth now work upon that object by desire, which is as it were a motion towards the end as yet unobtained; so likewise upon the same hereafter received it shall work also by love. "Appetitus inhiantis fit amor fruentis", saith St. Augustine: "The longing disposition of them that thirst is changed into the sweet affection of them that taste and are replenished" [*On the Trinity*, IX]. Whereas we now love the thing that is good, but good especially in respect of benefit unto us; we shall then love the thing that is good, only or principally for the goodness of beauty in itself. The soul being in this sort, as it is active, perfected by love of that infinite good, shall, as it is receptive, be also perfected with those supernatural passions of joy, peace, and delight. All this endless and everlasting [Matthew xxv.46]. Which perpetuity, in regard whereof our blessedness is termed "a crown which withereth not" [2 Tim. iv.8; 1 Peter v.4], doth neither depend

upon the nature of the thing itself, nor proceed from any natural necessity that our souls should so exercise themselves for ever in beholding and loving God, but from the will of God, which doth both freely perfect our nature in so high a degree, and continue it so perfected. Under Man, no creature in the world is capable of felicity and bliss. First, because their chiefest perfection consisteth in that which is best for them, and not in that which is simply best, as ours doth. Secondly, because whatsoever external perfection they tend unto, it is not better than themselves, as ours is. How just occasion have we therefore even in this respect with the Prophet to admire the goodness of God! "Lord, what is man, that thou shouldst exalt him above the works of thy hand" [Psalm viii.4], so far as to make thyself the inheritance of his rest and the substance of his felicity?

[4] Now if men had not naturally this desire to be happy, how were it possible that all men should have it? All men have. Therefore this desire in man is natural. It is not in our power not to do the same; how should it then be in our power to do it coldly or remissly? So that our desire being natural is also in that degree of earnestness whereunto nothing can be added. And is it probable that God should frame the hearts of all men so desirous of that which no man may obtain? It is an axiom of nature that natural desire cannot utterly be frustrate. This desire of ours being natural should be frustrate, if that which may satisfy the same were a thing impossible for man to aspire unto. Man doth seek a triple perfection: first a sensual, consisting in those things which very life itself requireth either as necessary supplements, or as beauties and ornaments thereof; then an intellectual, consisting in those things which none underneath man is either capable of or acquainted with; lastly a spiritual and divine, consisting in those things whereunto we tend by supernatural means here, but cannot here attain unto them.[1] They that make the first of these three the scope of their whole life, are said by the Apostle to have no god but only their belly, to be earthly-minded men [Phil. iii.19]. Unto the second they bend themselves, who seek

1   Aristotle, *Nicomachean Ethics*, I.5.

especially to excel in all such knowledge and virtue as doth most commend men. To this branch belongeth the law of moral and civil perfection. That there is somewhat higher than either of these two, no other proof doth need than the very process of man's desire, which being natural should be frustrate, if there were not some farther thing wherein it might rest at the length contented, which in the former it cannot do. For man doth not seem to rest satisfied, either with fruition of that wherewith his life is preserved, or with performance of such actions as advance him most deservedly in estimation; but doth further covet, yea oftentimes manifestly pursue with great sedulity and earnestness, that which cannot stand him in any stead for vital use; that which exceedeth the reach of sense; yea somewhat above capacity of reason, somewhat divine and heavenly, which with hidden exultation it rather surmiseth than conceiveth; somewhat it seeketh, and what that is directly it knoweth not, yet very intentive desire thereof doth so incite it, that all other known delights and pleasures are laid aside, they give place to the search of this but only suspected desire. If the soul of man did serve only to give him being in this life, then things appertaining unto this life would content him, as we see they do other creatures; which creatures enjoying what they live by seek no further, but in this contentation do shew a kind of acknowledgement that there is no higher good which doth any way belong unto them. With us it is otherwise. For although the beauties, riches, honours, sciences, virtues, and perfections of all men living, were in the present possession of one; yet somewhat beyond and above all this there would still be sought and earnestly thirsted for. So that Nature even in this life doth plainly claim and call for a more divine perfection than either of these two that have been mentioned.

[5] This last and highest estate of perfection whereof we speak is received of men in the nature of a Reward [Matthew v.12]. Rewards do always presuppose such duties performed as are rewardable. Our natural means therefore unto blessedness are our works; nor is it possible that Nature should ever find any other way to salvation than only this. But examine the works

which we do, and since the first foundation of the world what one can say, My ways are pure? Seeing then all flesh is guilty of that for which God hath threatened eternally to punish, what possibility is there this way to be saved? There resteth therefore either no way unto salvation, or if any, then surely a way which is supernatural, a way which could never have entered into the heart of man as much as once to conceive or imagine, if God himself had not revealed it extraordinarily. For which cause we term it the Mystery or secret way of salvation. And therefore St. Ambrose in this matter appealeth justly from man to God, "Cœli mysterium doceat me Deus qui condidit, non homo qui sepisum ignoravit: – Let God himself that made me, let not man that knows not himself, be my instructor concerning the mystical way to heaven".[1] "When men of excellent wit," saith Lactantius, "had wholly betaken themselves unto study, after farewell bidden unto all kind as well of private as public action, they spared no labour that might be spent in the search of truth; holding it a thing of much more price to seek and to find out the reason of all affairs as well divine as human, than to stick fast in the toil of piling up riches and gathering together heaps of honours. Howbeit, they both did fail of their purpose, and got not as much as to quite their charges; because truth which is the secret of the Most High God, whose proper handy-work all things are, cannot be compassed with that wit and those senses which are our own. For God and man should be very near neighbours, if man's cogitations were able to take a survey of the counsels and appointments of that Majesty everlasting. Which being utterly impossible, that the eye of man by itself should look into the bosom of divine Reason; God did not suffer him being desirous of the light of wisdom to stray any longer up and down, and with bootless expense of travail to wander in darkness that had no passage to get out by. His eyes at the length God did open, and bestow upon him the knowledge of the truth by way of Donative, to the end that man might both be clearly convicted of folly, and being through error out of the way, have the path that leadeth unto

1 Ambrose, *Against Symmachus* Letter 18.

immortality laid plain before him." Thus far Lactantius Firmianus, to shew that God himself is the teacher of the truth, whereby is made known the supernatural way of salvation and law for them to live in that shall be saved. In the natural path of everlasting life the first beginning is that ability of doing good, which God in the day of man's creation endued him with; from hence obedience unto the will of his Creator, absolute righteousness and integrity in all his actions; and last of all the justice of God rewarding the worthiness of his deserts with the crown of eternal glory. Had Adam continued in his first estate, this had been the way of life unto him and all his posterity. Wherein I confess notwithstanding with the wittiest of the school-divines, "That if we speak of strict justice, God could no way have been bound to requite man's labours in so large and ample a manner as human felicity doth import; inasmuch as the dignity of this exceedeth so far the other's value. But be it that God of his great liberality had determined in lieu of man's endeavours to bestow the same by the rule of that justice which best beseemeth him, namely, the justice of one that requiteth nothing mincingly, but all with pressed and heaped and even over-enlarged measure; yet could it never hereupon necessarily be gathered, that such justice should add to the nature of that reward the property of everlasting continuance; sith possession of bliss, though it should be but for a moment, were an abundant retribution".[1] But we are not now to enter into this consideration, how gracious and bountiful our good God might still appear in so rewarding the sons of men, albeit they should exactly perform whatsoever duty their nature bindeth them unto. Howsoever God did propose this reward, we that were to be rewarded must have done that which is required at our hands; we failing in the one, it were in nature an impossibility that the other should be looked for. The light of nature is never able to find out any way of obtaining the reward of bliss, but by performing exactly the duties and works of righteousness.

[6] From salvation therefore and life all flesh being excluded

1   Duns Scotus, IV.49.

this way, behold how the wisdom of God hath revealed a way mystical and supernatural, a way directing unto the same end of life by a course which groundeth itself upon the guiltiness of sin, and through sin desert of condemnation and death. For in this way the first thing is the tender compassion of God respecting us drowned and swallowed up in misery; the next is redemption out of the same by the precious death and merit of a mighty Saviour, which hath witnessed of himself, saying, "I am the way" [John xiv.6], the way that leadeth us from misery into bliss. This supernatural way had God in himself prepared before all worlds. The way of supernatural duty which to us he hath prescribed, our Saviour in the Gospel of St. John doth note, terming it by an excellency, The Work of God, "This is the work of God, that ye believe in him whom he hath sent" [John vi.29]. Not that God doth require nothing unto happiness at the hands of men saving only a naked belief (for hope and charity we may not exclude); but that without belief all other things are as nothing, and it the ground of those other divine virtues.

Concerning Faith, the principal object whereof is that eternal Verity which hath discovered the treasures of hidden wisdom in Christ; concerning Hope, the highest object whereof is that ever-lasting Goodness which in Christ doth quicken the dead; concerning Charity, the final object whereof is that incomprehensible Beauty which shineth in the countenance of Christ the Son of the living God: concerning these virtues, the first of which beginning here with a weak apprehension of things not seen, endeth with the intuitive vision of God in the world to come; the second beginning here with a trembling expectation of things far removed and as yet but only heard of, endeth with real and actual fruition of that which no tongue can express; the third beginning here with a weak inclination of heart towards him unto whom we are not able to approach, endeth with endless union, the mystery whereof is higher than the reach of the thoughts of men; concerning that Faith, Hope, and Charity, without which there can be no salvation, was there ever any mention made saving only in that law which God himself hath from heaven revealed? There is not in the world a syllable muttered with certain truth

concerning any of these three, more than hath been supernaturally received from the mouth of the eternal God.

Laws therefore concerning these things are supernatural, both
in respect of the manner of delivering them, which is divine; and
also in regard of the things delivered, which are such as have
not in nature any cause from which they flow, but were by the
voluntary appointment of God ordained besides the course of
nature, to rectify nature's obliquity withal.   (I.xi)

18   THE SUFFICIENCY OF SCRIPTURE

XIV. Although the Scripture of God therefore be stored with
infinite variety of matter in all kinds, although it abound with all
sorts of laws, yet the principal intent of Scripture is to deliver the
laws of duties supernatural. Oftentimes it hath been in very solemn manner disputed, whether all things necessary unto salvation be necessarily set down in the Holy Scriptures or no. If we
define that necessary unto salvation, whereby the way to salvation is in any sort made more plain, apparent, and easy to be
known; then is there no part of true philosophy, no art of account,
no kind of science rightly so called, but the Scripture must contain
it. If only those things be necessary, as surely none else are,
without the knowledge and practice whereof it is not the will
and pleasure of God to make any ordinary grant of salvation; it
may be notwithstanding and oftentimes hath been demanded,
how the books of Holy Scripture contain in them all necessary
things, when of things necessary the very chiefest is to know
what books we are bound to esteem holy; which point is confessed impossible for the Scripture itself to teach. Whereunto we
may answer with truth, that there is not in the world any art or
science, which proposing unto itself an end (as every one doth
some end or other) hath been therefore thought defective, if it
have not delivered simply whatsoever is needful to the same end;
but all kinds of knowledge have their certain bounds and limits;
each of them presupposeth many necessary things learned in

other sciences and known beforehand. He that should take upon him to teach men how to be eloquent in pleading causes, must needs deliver unto them whatsoever precepts are requisite unto that end; otherwise he doth not the thing which he taketh upon him. Seeing then no man can plead eloquently unless he be able first to speak; it followeth that ability of speech is in this case a thing most necessary. Notwithstanding every man would think it ridiculous, that he which undertaketh by writing to instruct an orator should therefore deliver all the precepts of grammar; because his profession is to deliver precepts necessary unto eloquent speech, yet so that they which are to receive them be taught beforehand so much of that which is thereunto necessary, as comprehendeth the skill of speaking. In like sort, albeit Scripture do profess to contain in it all things that are necessary unto salvation; yet the meaning cannot be simply of all things which are necessary, but all things that are necessary in some certain kind or form; as all things which are necessary, and either could not at all or could not easily be known by the light of natural discourse; all things which are necessary to be known that we may be saved, but known with presupposal of knowledge concerning certain principles whereof it receiveth us already persuaded, and then instructeth us in all the residue that are necessary. In the number of these principles one is the sacred authority of Scripture. Being therefore persuaded by other means that these Scriptures are the oracles of God, themselves do then teach us the rest, and lay before us all the duties which God requireth at our hands as necessary unto salvation.

[2] Further, there hath been some doubt likewise, whether *containing in Scripture* do import express setting down in plain terms, or else *comprehending* in such sort that by reason we may from thence conclude all things which are necessary. Against the former of these two constructions instance hath sundry ways been given. For our belief in the Trinity, the co-eternity of the Son of God with his Father, the proceeding of the Spirit from the Father and the Son, the duty of baptizing infants: these with such other principal points, the necessity whereof is by none denied, are notwithstanding in Scripture nowhere to be found by express

literal mention, only deduced they are out of Scripture by collection. This kind of comprehension in Scripture being therefore received, still there is doubt how far we are to proceed by collection, before the full and complete measure of things necessary be made up. For let us not think that as long as the world doth endure the wit of man shall be able to sound the bottom of that which may be concluded out of the Scripture; especially if "things contained by collection" do so far extend, as to draw in whatsoever may be at any time out of Scripture but probably and conjecturally surmised. But let *necessary* collection be made requisite, and we may boldly deny, that of all those things which at this day are with so great necessity urged upon this church under the name of reformed church-discipline, there is any one which their books hitherto have made manifest to be contained in the Scripture: Let them, if they can, allege but one properly belonging to their cause, and not common to them and us, and shew the deduction thereof out of Scripture to be necessary.

[3] It hath been already shewed, how all things necessary unto salvation in such sort as before we have maintained must needs be possible for men to know; and that many things are in such sort necessary, the knowledge whereof is by the light of Nature impossible to be attained. Whereupon it followeth that either all flesh is excluded from possibility of salvation, which to think were most barbarous; or else that God hath by supernatural means revealed the way of life so far forth as doth suffice. For this cause God hath so many times and ways spoken to the sons of men. Neither hath he by speech only, but by writing also, instructed and taught his Church. The cause of writing hath been to the end that things by him revealed unto the world might have the longer continuance, and the greater certainty of assurance, by how much that which standeth on record hath in both those respects preeminence above that which passeth from hand to hand, and hath no pens but the tongues, no books but the ears of men to record it. The several books of Scripture having had each some several occasion and particular purpose which caused them to be written, the contents thereof are according to the exigence of that special end whereunto they are intended. Here-

upon it groweth that every book of Holy Scripture doth take out
of all kinds of truth, natural [Eph. v.29], historical [2 Timothy
iii.8], foreign [Titus i.12], supernatural [2 Peter ii.4], so much as
the matter handled requireth.

Now forasmuch as there hath been reason alleged sufficient
to conclude, that all things necessary unto salvation must be made
known, and that God himself hath therefore revealed his will,
because otherwise men could not have known so much as is
necessary; his surceasing to speak to the world, since the publishing of the Gospel of Jesus Christ and the delivery of the same in
writing, is unto us a manifest token that the way of salvation is
now sufficiently opened, and that we need no other means for
our full instruction than God hath already furnished us withal.

[4] The main drift of the whole New Testament is that which
St. John setteth down as the purpose of his own history; "These
things are written, that ye might believe that Jesus is Christ the
Son of God, and that in believing ye might have life through his
name" [John xx.31]. The drift of the Old that which the Apostle
mentioned to Timothy, "The Holy Scriptures are able to make
thee wise unto salvation" [2 Tim. iii.15]. So that the general end
both of Old and New is one; the difference between them consisting in this, that the Old did make wise by teaching salvation
through Christ that should come, the New by teaching that Christ
the Saviour is come, and that Jesus whom the Jews did crucify,
and whom God did raise again from the dead, is he. When the
Apostle therefore affirmeth unto Timothy, that the Old was able
to make him wise to salvation, it was not his meaning that the
Old alone can do this unto us which live sithence the publication
of the New. For he speaketh with presupposal of the doctrine of
Christ known also unto Timothy; and therefore first it is said,
"Continue thou in those things which thou hast learned and art
persuaded, knowing of whom thou hast been taught them" [2
Tim. iii.14]. Again, those Scriptures he granteth were able to
make him wise to salvation; but he addeth, "through the faith
which is in Christ" [2 Tim. iii.15]. Wherefore without the doctrine
of the New Testament teaching that Christ hath wrought the
redemption of the world, which redemption the Old did fore-

shew he should work, it is not the former alone which can on our behalf perform so much as the Apostle doth avouch, who presupposeth this when he magnifieth that so highly. And as his words concerning the books of ancient Scripture do not take place but with presupposal of the Gospel of Christ embraced; so our own words also, when we extol the complete sufficiency of the whole entire body of the Scripture, must in like sort be understood with this caution, that the benefit of nature's light be not thought excluded as unnecessary, because the necessity of a diviner light is magnified.

[5] There is in Scripture therefore no defect, but that any man, what place or calling soever he hold in the Church of God, may have thereby the light of his natural understanding so perfected, that the one being relieved by the other, there can want no part of needful instruction unto any good work which God himself requireth, be it natural or supernatural, belonging simply unto men as men, or unto men as they are united in whatsoever kind of society. It sufficeth therefore that Nature and Scripture do serve in such full sort, that they both jointly, and not severally either of them, be so complete, that unto everlasting felicity we need not the knowledge of any thing more than these two may easily furnish our minds with on all sides; and therefore they which add traditions, as a part of supernatural necessary truth, have not the truth, but are in error. For they only plead, that whatsoever God revealeth as necessary for all Christian men to do or believe, the same we ought to embrace, whether we have received it by writing or otherwise; which no man denieth: when that which they should confirm, who claim so great reverence unto traditions, is, that the same traditions are necessarily to be acknowledged divine and holy. For we do not reject them only because they are not in the Scripture, but because they are neither in Scripture, nor can otherwise sufficiently by any reason be proved to be of God. That which is of God, and may be evidently proved to be so, we deny not but it hath in his kind, although unwritten, yet the selfsame force and authority with the written laws of God. It is by ours acknowledged, "that the Apostles did in every church institute and ordain some rites and customs serving

for the seemliness of church-regiment, which rites and customs they have not committed unto writing".[1] Those rites and customs being known to be apostolical, and having the nature of things changeable, were no less to be accounted of in the Church than other things of the like degree; that is to say, capable in like sort of alteration, although set down in the Apostles' writings. For both being known to be apostolical, it is not the manner of delivering them unto the Church, but the author from whom they proceed, which doth give them their force and credit.

(I.xiv)

19   DIVINE LAWS AND THEIR INTERPRETATION

XV. Laws being imposed either by each man upon himself, or by a public society upon the particulars thereof, or by all the nations of men upon every several society, or by the Lord himself upon any or every of these; there is not amongst these four kinds any one but containeth sundry both natural and positive laws. Impossible it is but that they should fall into a number of gross errors, who only take such laws for positive as have been made or invented of men, and holding this position hold also, that all positive and none but positive laws are mutable. Laws natural do always bind; laws positive not so, but only after they have been expressly and wittingly imposed. Laws positive there are in every of those kinds before mentioned. As in the first kind the promises which we have passed unto men, and the vows we have made unto God; for these are laws which we tie ourselves unto, and till we have so tied ourselves they bind us not. Laws positive in the second kind are such as the civil constitutions peculiar unto each particular commonweal. In the third kind the law of Heraldry in war is positive: and in the last all the judicials which God gave unto the people of Israel to observe. And although

1   Whitaker, *Against Bellarmine*, Qn.6, 6.

no laws but positive be mutable, yet all are not mutable which be positive. Positive laws are either permanent or else changeable, according as the matter itself is concerning which they were first made. Whether God or man be the maker of them, alteration they so far forth admit, as the matter doth exact.

[2] Laws that concern supernatural duties are all positive, and either concern men supernaturally as men, or else as parts of a supernatural society, which society we call the Church. To concern men as men supernaturally is to concern them as duties which belong of necessity to all, and yet could not have been known by any to belong unto them, unless God had opened them himself, inasmuch as they do not depend upon any natural ground at all out of which they may be deduced, but are appointed of God to supply the defect of those natural ways of salvation, by which we are not now able to attain thereunto. The Church being a supernatural society doth differ from natural societies in this, that the persons unto whom we associate ourselves, in the one are men simply considered as men, but they to whom we be joined in the other, are God, Angels, and holy men. Again the Church being both a society and a society supernatural, although as it is a society it have the selfsame original grounds which other politic societies have, namely, the natural inclination which all men have unto sociable life, and consent to some certain bond of association, which bond is the law that appointeth what kind of order they shall be associated in: yet unto the Church as it is a society supernatural this is peculiar, that part of the bond of their association which belong to the Church of God must be a law supernatural, which God himself hath revealed concerning that kind of worship which his people shall do unto him. The substance of the service of God therefore, so far forth as it hath in it any thing more than the Law of Reason doth teach, may not be invented of men, as it is amongst the heathens, but must be received from God himself, as always it hath been in the Church, saving only when the Church hath been forgetful of her duty.

[3] Wherefore to end with a general rule concerning all the laws which God hath tied men unto: those laws divine that

belong, whether naturally or supernaturally, either to men as
men, or to men as they live in politic society, or to men as they
are of that politic society which is the Church, without any further
respect had unto any such variable accident as the state of men
and of societies of men and of the Church itself in this world is
subject unto; all laws that so belong unto men, they belong for
ever, yea although they be Positive Laws, unless being positive
God himself which made them alter them. The reason is, because
the subject or matter of laws in general is thus far forth constant:
which matter is that for the ordering whereof laws were instituted, and being instituted are not changeable without cause,
neither can they have cause of change, when that which gave
them their first institution remaineth for ever one and the same.
On the other side, laws that were made for men or societies or
churches, in regard of their being such as they do not always
continue, but may perhaps be clean otherwise a while after, and
so may require to be otherwise ordered than before; the laws of
God himself which are of this nature, no man endued with common sense will ever deny to be of a different constitution from
the former, in respect of the one's constancy and the mutability
of the other. And this doth seem to have been the very cause
why St. John doth so peculiarly term the doctrine that teacheth
salvation by Jesus Christ, *Evangelium æternum*, "an eternal Gospel" [Revelation xiv.6]; because there can be no reason wherefore
the publishing thereof should be taken away, and any other
instead of it proclaimed, as long as the world doth continue:
whereas the whole law of rites and ceremonies, although delivered with so great solemnity, is notwithstanding clean abrogated, inasmuch as it had but temporary cause of God's ordaining
it.

[4] But that we may at the length conclude this first general
introduction unto the nature and original birth, as of all other
laws, so likewise of those which the sacred Scripture containeth,
concerning the Author whereof even infidels have confessed that
He can neither err nor deceive: albeit about things easy and manifest unto all men by common sense there needeth no higher
consultation; because as a man whose wisdom is in weighty

affairs admired would take it in some disdain to have his counsel
solemnly asked about a toy, so the meanness of some things is
such, that to search the Scripture of God for the ordering of them
were to derogate from the reverend authority and dignity of the
Scripture, no less than they do by whom Scriptures are in ordinary talk very idly applied unto vain and childish trifles: yet better
it were to be superstitious than profane; to take from thence our
direction even in all things great or small, than to wade through
matters of principal weight and moment, without ever caring
what the law of God hath either for or against our designs. Concerning the custom of the very Painims, thus much Strabe witnesseth: "Men that are civil do lead their lives after one common law
appointing them what to do. For that otherwise a multitude
should with harmony amongst themselves concur in the doing
of one thing, (for this is civilly to live), or that they should in any
sort manage community of life, it is not possible. Now laws or
statutes are of two sorts. For they are either received from gods,
or else from men. And our ancient predecessors did surely most
honour and reverence that which was from the gods; for which
cause consultation with oracles was a thing very usual and frequent in their times".[1] Did they make so much account of the
voice of their gods, which in truth were no gods; and shall we
neglect the precious benefit of conference with those oracles of
the true and living God, whereof so great store is left to the
Church, and whereunto there is so free, so plain, and so easy
access for all men? "By thy commandments" (this was David's
confession unto God) "thou hast made me wiser than mine
enemies". Again, "I have had more understanding than all my
teachers, because thy testimonies are my meditations" [Psalm
cxix.98]. What pains would not they have bestowed in the study
of these books, who travelled sea and land to gain the treasure
of some few days' talk with men whose wisdom the world did
make any reckoning of? That little which some of the heathens
did chance to hear, concerning such matter as the sacred Scripture
plentifully containeth, they did in wonderful sort affect; their

1 Strabo, *Geography*, XVI.31.

speeches as oft as they make mention thereof are strange, and such as themselves could not utter as they did other things, but still acknowledged that their wits, which did every where else conquer hardness, were with profoundness here over-matched. Wherefore seeing that God hath endued us with sense, to the end that we might perceive such things as this present life doth need; and with reason, lest that which sense cannot reach unto, being both now and also in regard of a future estate hereafter necessary to be known, should lie obscure; finally, with the heavenly support of prophetical revelation, which doth open those hidden mysteries that reason could never have been able to find out, or to have known the necessity of them unto our everlasting good: use we the precious gifts of God unto his glory and honour that gave them, seeking by all means to know what the will of our God is; what righteous before him; in his sight what holy, perfect, and good, that we may truly and faithfully do it.   (I.xv)

20   SUMMARY AND THE RELATION OF LAW
TO ECCLESIASTICAL POLITY

XVI. Thus far therefore we have endeavoured in part to open, of what nature and force laws are, according unto their several kinds; the law which God with himself hath eternally set down to follow in his own works; the law which he hath made for his creatures to keep; the law of natural and necessary agents; the law which angels in heaven obey; the law whereunto by the light of reason men find themselves bound in that they are men; the law which they make by composition for multitudes and politic societies of men to be guided by; the law which belongeth unto each nation; the law that concerneth the fellowship of all; and lastly the law which God himself hath supernaturally revealed. It might peradventure have been more popular and more plausible to vulgar ears, if this first discourse had been spent in extolling the force of laws, in shewing the great necessity of them when they are good, and in aggravating their offence by whom public laws are injuriously traduced. But forasmuch as with such kind of matter the passions of men are rather stirred one way or other, than their knowledge any way set forward unto the trial of that whereof there is doubt made; I have therefore turned aside from that beaten path, and chosen though a less easy yet a more profitable way in regard of the end we propose. Lest therefore any man should marvel whereunto all these things tend, the drift and purpose of all is this, even to shew in what manner, as every good and perfect gift, so this very gift of good and perfect laws is derived from the Father of lights; to teach men a reason why just and reasonable laws are of so great force, of so great use in the world; and to inform their minds with some method of reducing the laws whereof there is present controversy unto their first original causes, that so it may be in every particular ordinance thereby the better discerned, whether the same be reasonable, just, and righteous, or no. Is there any thing which can either be throughly understood or soundly judged of, till the very first causes and principles from which originally it springeth be made manifest? If all parts of knowledge have been thought by wise men to be then most orderly delivered and proceeded in, when they are drawn to their first original;[1] seeing that our whole question concerneth the quality of ecclesiastical laws, let it not seem a labour superfluous that in the entrance thereunto all these several kinds of laws have been considered, inasmuch as they all concur as principles, they all have their forcible operations therein, although not all in like apparent and manifest manner. By means whereof it cometh to pass that the force which they have is not observed of many.

[2] Easier a great deal it is for men by law to be taught what they ought to do, than instructed how to judge as they should do of law: the one being a thing which belongeth generally unto all, the other such as none but the wiser and more judicious sort can perform. Yea, the wisest are always touching this point the readiest to acknowledge, that soundly to judge of a law is the

1 Aristotle, *Physics*, I.i.

weightiest thing which any man can take upon him.[1] But if we will give judgment of the laws under which we live; first let that law eternal be always before our eyes, as being of principal force and moment to breed in religious minds a dutiful estimation of all laws, the use and benefit whereof we see; because there can be no doubt but that laws apparently good are (as it were) things copied out of the very tables of that high everlasting law; even as the book of that law hath said concerning itself, "By me kings reign, and" by me "princes decree justice" [Proverbs viii.15]. . . .

[8] Wherefore that here we may briefly end: of Law there can be no less acknowledged, than that her seat is the bosom of God, her voice the harmony of the world: all things in heaven and earth do her homage, the very least as feeling her care, and the greatest as not exempted from her power, both Angels and men and creatures of what condition soever, though each in different sort and manner, yet all with uniform consent, admiring her as the mother of their peace and joy.   (I.xvi.1-2, 8)

1   Aristotle, *Ethics*, X.10.

Book II

Books II and III of *Ecclesiastical Polity* are concerned with Puritan claims that Scripture contains sufficient guidance on all things human (II) and that it must therefore contain a perfect and unalterable form of church order and government (III). As part of his refutation of the first assertion, Hooker argues that Scripture is not the sole and exclusive mode chosen by God to reveal His will to man (21), nor is it to be the sole and exclusive ground of man's faith (22). Indeed, to claim such is to demean human authority given by God and expressed through such faculties as reason, will and conscience (23).

21 SCRIPTURE NOT MAN'S ONLY LAW

... Scripture is not the only law whereby God hath opened his will touching all things that may be done, but there are other kinds of laws which notify the will of God, as in the former book hath been proved at large: nor is there any law of God, whereunto he doth not account our obedience his glory. "Do therefore all things unto the glory of God (saith the Apostle), be inoffensive both to Jews and Grecians and the Church of God; even as I please all men in all things, not seeking mine own commodity, but many's, that they may be saved" [1 Cor.x.31-3]. In the least thing done disobediently towards God, or offensively against the good of men, whose benefit we ought to seek for as for our own, we plainly shew that we do not acknowledge God to be such as indeed he is, and consequently that we glorify him not. This the blessed Apostle teacheth; but doth any Apostle teach, that we cannot glorify God otherwise, than only in doing what we find that God in Scripture commandeth us to do?   (II.ii.2)

22 SCRIPTURE NOT THE ONLY GROUND OF FAITH

IV. But to come unto that which of all other things in Scripture is most stood upon; that place of St. Paul they say is "of all other most clear, where speaking of those things which are called indifferent, in the end he concludeth, That 'whatsoever is not of faith is sin'. But faith is not but in respect of the Word of God. Therefore whatsoever is not done by the Word of God is sin". Whereunto we answer, that albeit the name of Faith being properly and strictly taken, it must needs have reference unto some uttered word as the object of belief: nevertheless sith the ground of credit is the credibility of things credited; and things are made credible, either by the known condition and quality of the utterer, or by the manifest likelihood of truth which they have in themselves; hereupon it riseth that whatsoever we are persuaded of, the same we are generally said to believe. In which generality the object of faith may not so narrowly be restrained, as if the same did extend no further than to the only Scriptures of God. "Though", saith our Saviour, "ye believe not me, believe my works, that ye may know and believe that the Father is in me and I in him" [John x.38]. "The other disciples said unto Thomas, We have seen the Lord"; but his answer unto them was, "Except I see in his hands the print of the nails, and put my finger into them, I will not believe" [John xx.25]. Can there be any thing more plain than that which by these two sentences appeareth, namely, that there may be a certain belief grounded upon other assurance than Scripture: any thing more clear, than that we are said not only to believe the things which we know by another's relation, but even whatsoever we are certainly persuaded of, whether it be by reason or by sense?

[2] Forasmuch therefore as it is granted that St. Paul doth mean nothing else by Faith, but only "a full persuasion that that which we do is well done"; against which kind of faith or persuasion as St. Paul doth count it sin to enterprise any thing, so likewise "some of the very heathen have taught, as Tully, 'That nothing ought to be done whereof thou doubtest whether it be right or wrong;[1] whereby it appeareth that even those which had no knowledge of the word of God did see much of the equity of this which the Apostle requireth of a Christian man"; I hope we shall

1   Cicero, *De Officiis*, I.9.

not seem altogether unnecessarily to doubt of the soundness of
their opinion, who think simply that nothing but only the word
of God can give us assurance in any thing we are to do, and
resolve us that we do well. For might not the Jews have been
fully persuaded that they did well to think (if they had so thought)
that in Christ God the Father was, although the only ground of
their faith had been the wonderful works they saw him do? Might
not, yea, did not Thomas fully in the end persuade himself, that
he did well to think that body which now was raised to be the
same which had been crucified? That which gave Thomas this
assurance was his sense; "Thomas, because thou hast seen, thou
believest", saith our Saviour [John xx.29]. What Scripture had
Tully for this assurance? Yet I nothing doubt but that they who
allege him think he did well to set down in writing a thing so
consonant unto truth. Finally, we all believe that the Scriptures
of God are sacred, and that they have proceeded from God; ourselves we assure that we do right well in so believing. We have
for this point a demonstration sound and infallible. But it is not
the word of God which doth or possibly can assure us, that we
do well to think it his word. For if any one book of Scripture did
give testimony to all, yet still that Scripture which giveth credit
to the rest would require another Scripture to give credit unto it,
neither could we ever come unto any pause whereon to rest our
assurance this way; so that unless beside Scripture there were
something which might assure us that we do well, we could not
think we do well, no not in being assured that Scripture is a
sacred and holy rule of well-doing.   (II.iv.1-2)

23   EXCLUSIVE RELIANCE ON SCRIPTURE
DEMEANS HUMAN REASON

VII. An earnest desire to draw all things unto the determination
of bare and naked Scripture hath caused here much pains to be
taken in abating the estimation and credit of man. Which if we
labour to maintain as far as truth and reason will bear, let not any

think that we travail about a matter not greatly needful. For the scope of all their pleading against man's authority is, to overthrow such orders, laws, and constitutions in the Church, as depending thereupon if they should therefore be taken away, would peradventure leave neither face nor memory of Church to continue long in the world, the world especially being such as now it is. That which they have in this case spoken I would for brevity's sake let pass, but that the drift of their speech being so dangerous, their words are not to be neglected.

[2] Wherefore to say that simply an argument taken from man's authority doth hold no way, "neither affirmatively nor negatively", is hard. By a man's authority we here understand the force which his word hath for the assurance of another's mind that buildeth upon it; as the Apostle somewhat did upon their report of the house of Chloe [1 Cor. i.11]; and the Samaritans in a matter of far greater moment upon the report of a simple woman. For so it is said in St. John's Gospel, "Many of the Samaritans of that city believed in him for the saying of the woman, which testified, He hath told me all things that ever I did" [John iv.39].

The strength of man's authority is affirmatively such that the weightiest affairs in the world depend thereon. In judgment and justice are not hereupon proceedings grounded? Saith not the Law that "in the mouth of two or three witnesses every word shall be confirmed?" [Deut. xix.15; Matthew xviii.16]. This the law of God would not say, if there were in a man's testimony no force at all to prove any thing.

And if it be admitted that in matter of fact there is some credit to be given to the testimony of man, but not in matter of opinion and judgment; we see the contrary both acknowledged and universally practised also throughout the world. The sentences of wise and expert men were never but highly esteemed. Let the title of a man's right be called in question; are we not bold to rely and build upon the judgment of such as are famous for their skill in the laws of this land? In matter of state the weight many times of some one man's authority is thought reason sufficient, even to sway over whole nations.

And this not only "with the simpler sort"; but the learneder and wiser we are, the more such arguments in some cases prevail with us. The reason why the simpler sort are moved with authority is the conscience of their own ignorance; whereby it cometh to pass that having learned men in admiration, they rather fear to dislike them than know wherefore they should allow and follow their judgments. Contrariwise with them that are skilful authority is much more strong and forcible; because they only are able to discern how just cause there is why to some men's authority so much should be attributed. For which cause the name of Hippocrates (no doubt) were more effectual to persuade even such men as Galen himself, than to move a silly empiric. So that the very selfsame argument in this kind which doth but induce the vulgar sort to like, may constrain the wiser to yield. And therefore not orators only with the people, but even the very profoundest disputers in all faculties have hereby often with the best learned prevailed most.

As for arguments taken from human authority and that negatively; for example sake, if we should think the assembling of the people of God together by the sound of a bell, the presenting of infants at the holy font by such as commonly we call their godfathers, or any other the like received custom, to be impious, because some men of whom we think very reverently have in their books and writings nowhere mentioned or taught that such things should be in the Church; this reasoning were subject unto just reproof, it were but feeble, weak, and unsound. Notwithstanding even negatively an argument from human authority may be strong, as namely thus: The Chronicles of England mention no more than only six kings bearing the name of Edward since the time of the last conquest; therefore it cannot be there should be more. So that if the question be of the authority of a man's testimony, we cannot simply avouch either that affirmatively it doth not any way hold; or that it hath only force to induce the simpler sort, and not to constrain men of understanding and ripe judgment to yield assent; or that negatively it hath in it no strength at all. For unto every of these the contrary is most plain.

[3] Neither doth that which is alleged concerning the infirmity

of men overthrow or disprove this. Men are blinded with ignorance and error; many things may escape them, and in many things they may be deceived; yea, those things which they do know they may either forget, or upon sundry indirect considerations let pass; and although themselves do not err, yet may they through malice or vanity even of purpose deceive others. Howbeit infinite cases there are wherein all these impediments and lets are so manifestly excluded, that there is no show or colour whereby any such exception may be taken, but that the testimony of man will stand as a ground of infallible assurance. That there is a city of Rome, that Pius Quintus and Gregory the Thirteenth and others have been Popes of Rome, I suppose we are certainly enough persuaded. The ground of our persuasion, who never saw the place nor persons beforenamed, can be nothing but man's testimony. Will any man here notwithstanding allege those mentioned human infirmities, as reasons why these things should be mistrusted or doubted of?

Yea, that which is more, utterly to infringe the force and strength of man's testimony were to shake the very fortress of God's truth. For whatsoever we believe concerning the salvation by Christ, although the Scripture be therein the ground of our belief; yet the authority of man is, if we mark it, the key which openeth the door of entrance into the knowledge of the Scripture. The Scripture could not teach us the things that are of God, unless we did credit men who have taught us that the words of Scripture do signify those things. Some way therefore, notwithstanding man's infirmity, yet his authority may enforce assent.

[4] Upon better advice and deliberation so much is perceived, and at the length confest; that arguments taken from the authority of men may not only so far forth in "human sciences"; which force be it never so small, doth shew that they are not utterly naught. But in "matters divine" it is still maintained stiffly, that they have no manner force at all. Howbeit, the very selfsame reason, which causeth to yield that they are of some force in the one, will at the length constrain also to acknowledge that they are not in the other altogether unforcible. For if the natural strength of man's wit may by experience and study attain unto

such ripeness in the knowledge of things human, that men in this respect may presume to build somewhat upon their judgment; what reason have we to think but that even in matters divine, the like wits furnished with necessary helps, exercised in Scripture with like diligence, and assisted with the grace of Almighty God, may grow unto so much perfection of knowledge, that men shall have just cause, when any thing pertinent unto faith and religion is doubted of, the more willingly to incline their minds towards that which the sentence of so grave, wise, and learned in that faculty shall judge most sound? For the controversy is of the weight of such men's judgments. Let it therefore be suspected; let it be taken as gross, corrupt, repugnant unto the truth, whatsoever concerning things divine above nature shall at any time be spoken as out of the mouths of mere natural men, which have not the eyes wherewith heavenly things are discerned. For this we contend not. But whom God hath endued with principal gifts to aspire unto knowledge by; whose exercises, labours, and divine studies he hath so blessed that the world for their great and rare skill that way hath them in singular admiration; may we reject even their judgment likewise, as being utterly of no moment? For mine own part, I dare not so lightly esteem of the Church, and of the principal pillars therein.

[5] The truth is, that the mind of man desireth evermore to know the truth according to the most infallible certainty which the nature of things can yield. The greatest assurance generally with all men is that which we have by plain aspect and intuitive beholding. Where we cannot attain unto this, there what appeareth to be true by strong and invincible demonstration, such as wherein it is not by any way possible to be deceived, thereunto the mind doth necessarily assent, neither is it in the choice thereof to do otherwise. And in case these both do fail, then which way greatest probability leadeth, thither the mind doth evermore incline. Scripture with Christian men being received as the Word of God; that for which we have probable, yea, that which we have necessary reason for, yea, that which we see with our eyes, is not thought so sure as that which the Scripture of God teacheth; because we hold that his speech

revealeth there what himself seeth, and therefore the strongest proof of all, and the most necessarily assented unto by us (which do thus receive the Scripture) is the Scripture. Now it is not required or can be exacted at our hands, that we should yield unto any thing other assent, than such as doth answer the evidence which is to be had of that we assent unto. For which cause even in matters divine, concerning some things we may lawfully doubt and suspend our judgment, inclining neither to one side nor other; as namely touching the time of the fall both of man and angels: of some things we may very well retain an opinion that they are probable and not unlikely to be true, as when we hold that men have their souls rather by creation than propagation, or that the Mother of our Lord lived always in the state of virginity as well after his birth as before (for of these two the one, her virginity before, is a thing which of necessity we must believe; the other, her continuance in the same state always, hath more likelihood of truth than the contrary); finally in all things then are our consciences best resolved, and in most agreeable sort unto God and nature settled, when they are so far persuaded as those grounds of persuasion which are to be had will bear.

Which thing I do so much the rather set down, for that I see how a number of souls are for want of right information in this point oftentimes grievously vexed. When bare and unbuilded conclusions are put into their minds, they finding not themselves to have thereof any great certainty, imagine that this proceedeth only from lack of faith, and that the Spirit of God doth not work in them as it doth in true believers; by this means their hearts are much troubled, they fall into anguish and perplexity: whereas the truth is, that how bold and confident soever we may be in words, when it cometh to the point of trial, such as the evidence is which the truth hath either in itself or through proof, such is the heart's assent thereunto; neither can it be stronger, being grounded as it should be.

I grant that proof derived from the authority of man's judgment is not able to work that assurance which doth grow by a stronger proof; and therefore although ten thousand general councils would set down one and the same definitive sentence concerning any point of religion whatsoever, yet one demonstrative reason alleged, or one manifest testimony cited from the mouth of God himself to the contrary, could not choose but overweigh them all; inasmuch as for them to have been deceived it is not impossible; it is, that demonstrative reason or testimony divine should deceive. Howbeit in defect of proof infallible, because the mind doth rather follow probable persuasions than approve the things that have in them no likelihood of truth at all; surely if a question concerning matter of doctrine were proposed, and on the one side no kind of proof appearing, there should on the other be alleged and shewed that so a number of the learnedest divines in the world have ever thought; although it did not appear what reason or what Scripture led them to be of that judgment, yet to their very bare judgment somewhat a reasonable man would attribute, notwithstanding the common imbecilities which are incident into our nature.

[6] And whereas it is thought, that especially with "the Church, and those that are called and persuaded of the authority of the Word of God, man's authority" with them especially "should not prevail"; it must and doth prevail even with them, yea with them especially, as far as equity requireth; and farther we maintain it not.[1] For men to be tied and led by authority, as it were with a kind of captivity of judgment, and though there be reason to the contrary not to listen unto it, but to follow like beasts the first in the herd, they know not nor care not whither, this were brutish. Again, that authority of men should prevail with men either against or above Reason, is no part of our belief. "Companies of learned men" be they never so great and reverend, are to yield unto Reason; the weight thereof is no whit prejudiced by the simplicity of his person which doth allege it, but being found to be sound and good, the bare opinion of men to the contrary must of necessity stoop and give place.

Irenæus, writing against Marcion, which held one God author of the Old Testament and another of the New, to prove that the Apostles preached the same God which was known before to the

1   Cartwright, II.21.

Jews, he copiously allegeth sundry their sermons and speeches uttered concerning that matter and recorded in Scripture. And lest any should be wearied with such store of allegations, in the end he concludeth, "While we labour for these demonstrations out of Scripture, and do summarily declare the things which many ways have been spoken, be contented quietly to hear, and do not think any speech tedious: Quoniam ostensiones quæ sunt in Scripturis non possunt ostendi nisi ex ipsis Scripturis; Because demonstrations that are in Scripture may not otherwise be shewed than by citing them out of the Scriptures themselves where they are". Which words make so little unto the purpose, that they seem as it were offended at him which hath called them thus solemnly forth to say nothing.

And concerning the verdict of Jerome; if no man, be he never so well learned, have after the Apostles any authority to publish new doctrine as from heaven, and to require the world's assent as unto truth received by prophetical revelation; doth this prejudice the credit of learned men's judgments in opening that truth, which by being conversant in the Apostles' writings they have themselves from thence learned?

St. Augustine exhorteth not to hear men, but to hearken what God speaketh. His purpose is not (I think) that we should stop our ears against his own exhortation, and therefore he cannot mean simply that audience should altogether be denied unto men, but either that if men speak one thing and God himself teach another, then he not they to be obeyed; or if they both speak the same thing, yet then also man's speech unworthy of hearing, not simply, but in comparison of that which proceedeth from the mouth of God.

"Yea, but we doubt what the will of God is". Are we in this case forbidden to hear what men of judgment think it to be? If not, then this allegation also might very well have been spared.

In that ancient strife which was between the catholic Fathers and Arians, Donatists, and others of like perverse and froward disposition, as long as to Fathers or councils alleged on the one side the like by the contrary side were opposed, impossible it was that ever the question should by this means grow unto any issue or end. The Scripture they both believed: the Scripture they knew could not give sentence on both sides; by Scripture the controversy between them was such as might be determined. In this case what madness was it with such kinds of proofs to nourish their contention, when there were such effectual means to end all controversy that was between them! Hereby therefore it doth not as yet appear, that an argument of authority of man affirmatively is in matters divine nothing worth.

Which opinion being once inserted into the minds of the vulgar sort, what it may grow unto God knoweth. Thus much we see, it hath already made thousands so headstrong even in gross and palpable errors, that a man whose capacity will scarce serve him to utter five words in sensible manner blusheth not in any doubt concerning matter of Scripture to think his own bare *Yea* as good as the *Nay* of all the wise, grave, and learned judgments that are in the whole world: which insolency must be repressed, or it will be the very bane of Christian religion.

[7] Our Lord's disciples marking what speech he uttered unto them, and at the same time calling to mind a common opinion held by the Scribes, between which opinion and the words of their Master it seemeth unto them that there was some contradiction, which they could not themselves answer with full satisfaction of their own minds; the doubt they propose to our Saviour, saying, "Why then say the Scribes that Elias must first come?" [Matthew xvii.10]. They knew that the Scribes did err greatly, and that many ways even in matters of their own profession. They notwithstanding thought the judgment of the very Scribes in matters divine to be of some value; some probability they thought there was that Elias should come, inasmuch as the Scribes said it. Now no truth can contradict any truth; desirous therefore they were to be taught how both might stand together; that which they knew could not be false, because Christ spake it; and this which to them did seem true, only because the Scribes had said it. For the Scripture, from whence the Scribes did gather it, was not then in their heads. We do not find that our Saviour reproved them of error, for thinking the judgment of the Scribes to be worth the objecting, for esteeming it to be of any moment

or value in matters concerning God.

[8] We cannot therefore be persuaded that the will of God is, we should so far reject the authority of men as to reckon it nothing. No, it may be a question, whether they that urge us unto this be themselves so persuaded indeed. Men do sometimes bewray that by deeds, which to confess they are hardly drawn. Mark then if this be not general with all men for the most part. When the judgments of learned men are alleged against them, what do they but either elevate their credit, or oppose unto them the judgments of others as learned? Which thing doth argue that all men acknowledge in them some force and weight, for which they are loath the cause they maintain should be so much weakened as their testimony is available. Again, what reason is there why alleging testimonies as proofs, men give them some title of credit, honour, and estimation, whom they allege, unless beforehand it be sufficiently known who they are; what reason hereof but only a common ingrafted persuasion, that in some men there may be found such qualities as are able to countervail those exceptions which might be taken against them, and that such men's authority is not lightly to be shaken off?

[9] Shall I add further, that the force of arguments drawn from the authority of Scripture itself, as Scriptures commonly are alleged, shall (being sifted) be found to depend upon the strength of this so much despised and debased authority of man? Surely it doth, and that oftener than we are aware of. For although Scripture be of God, and therefore the proof which is taken from thence must needs be of all other most invincible; yet this strength it hath not, unless it avouch the selfsame thing for which it is brought. If there be either undeniable appearance that so it doth, or reason such as cannot deceive, then Scripture-proof (no doubt) in strength and value exceedeth all. But for the most part, even such as are readiest to cite for one thing five hundred sentences of holy Scripture; what warrant have they, that any one of them doth mean the thing for which it is alleged? Is not their surest ground most commonly, either some possible conjecture of their own, or the judgment of others taking those Scriptures as they do? Which notwithstanding to mean otherwise than they take

them, it is not still altogether impossible. So that now and then they ground themselves on human authority, even when they most pretend divine. Thus it fareth even clean throughout the whole controversy about that discipline which is so earnestly urged and laboured for. Scriptures are plentifully alleged to prove that the whole Christian world for ever ought to embrace it. Hereupon men term it *The discipline of God*. Howbeit examine, sift and resolve their alleged proofs, till you come to the very root from whence they spring, the heart wherein their strength lieth; and it shall clearly appear unto any man of judgment, that the most which can be inferred upon such plenty of divine testimonies is only this, That *some things* which they maintain, as far as *some men* can *probably conjecture*, do *seem* to have been out of Scripture *not absurdly* gathered. Is this a warrant sufficient for any man's conscience to build such proceedings upon, as have been and are put in ure for the stablishment of that cause?

[10] But to conclude, I would gladly understand how it cometh to pass, that they which so peremptorily do maintain that human authority is nothing worth are in the cause which they favour so careful to have the common sort of men persuaded, that the wisest, the godliest and the best learned in all Christendom are that way given, seeing they judge this to make nothing in the world for them. Again how cometh it to pass they cannot abide that authority should be alleged on the other side, if there be no force at all in authorities on one side or other? Wherefore labour they to strip their adversaries of such furniture as doth not help? Why take they such needless pains to furnish also their own cause with the like? If it be void and to no purpose that the names of men are so frequent in their books, what did move them to bring them in, or doth to suffer them there remaining? Ignorant I am not how this is salved, "They do it not but after the truth made manifest first by reason or by Scripture: they do it not but to control the enemies of truth, who bear themselves bold upon human authority making not for them but against them rather".[1] Which answers are nothing: for in what place or upon what

1   *Christian Letter*, p.8.

consideration soever it be they do it, were it in their own opinion of no force being done, they would undoubtedly refrain to do it.

VIII. But to the end it may more plainly appear what we are to judge of their sentences, and of the cause itself wherein they are alleged: first it may not well be denied, that all actions of men endued with the use of reason are generally either good or evil. For although it be granted that no action is properly termed good or evil unless it be voluntary; yet this can be no let to our former assertion, That all actions of men endued with the use of reason are generally either good or evil; because even those things are done voluntarily by us which other creatures do naturally, inasmuch as we might stay our doing of them if we would. Beasts naturally do take their food and rest when it offereth itself unto them. If men did so too, and could not do otherwise of themselves, there were no place for any such reproof as that of our Saviour Christ unto his disciples, "Could ye not watch with me one hour?" That which is voluntarily performed in things tending to the end, if it be well done, must needs be done with deliberate consideration of some reasonable cause wherefore we rather should do it than not. Whereupon it seemeth, that in such actions only those are said to be good or evil which are capable of deliberation: so that many things being hourly done by men, wherein they need not use with themselves any manner of consultation at all, it may perhaps hereby seem that well or ill-doing belongeth only to our weightier affairs, and to those deeds which are of so great importance that they require advice. But thus to determine were perilous, and peradventure unsound also. I do rather incline to think, that seeing all the unforced actions of men are voluntary, and all voluntary actions tending to the end have choice, and all choice presupposeth the knowledge of some cause wherefore we make it: where the reasonable cause of such actions so readily offereth itself that it needeth not to be sought for; in those things though we do not deliberate, yet they are of their nature apt to be deliberated on, in regard of the will, which may incline either way, and would not any one way bend itself, if there were not some apparent motive to lead it. Deliberation actual we use, when there is doubt what we should incline our wills unto. Where no doubt is, deliberation is not excluded as impertinent unto the thing, but as needless in regard of the agent, which seeth already what to resolve upon. It hath no apparent absurdity therefore in it to think, that all actions of men endued with the use of reason are generally either good or evil.

[2] Whatsoever is good, the same is also approved of God: and according unto the sundry degrees of goodness, the kinds of divine approbation are in like sort multiplied. Some things are good, yet in so mean a degree of goodness, that men are only not disproved nor disallowed of God for them. "No man hateth his own flesh" [Eph. v.29]. "If ye do good unto them that do so to you, the very publicans themselves do as much" [Matthew v.46]. "They are worse than infidels that have no care to provide for their own" [1 Tim. v.8]. In actions of this sort, the very light of Nature alone may discover that which is so far forth in the sight of God allowable.

[3] Some things in such sort are allowed, that they be also required as necessary unto salvation, by way of direct immediate and proper necessity final; so that without performance of them we cannot by ordinary course be saved, nor by any means be excluded from life observing them. In actions of this kind our chiefest direction is from Scripture, for Nature is no sufficient teacher what we should do that we may attain unto life everlasting. The unsufficiency of the light of Nature is by the light of Scripture so fully and so perfectly herein supplied, that further light than this hath added there doth not need unto that end.

[4] Finally some things, although not so required of necessity that to leave them undone excludeth from salvation, are notwithstanding of so great dignity and acceptation with God, that most ample reward in heaven is laid up for them. Hereof we have no commandment either in Nature or Scripture which doth exact them at our hands; yet those motives there are in both which draw most effectually our minds unto them. In this kind there is not the least action but it doth somewhat make to the accessory augmentation of our bliss. For which cause our Saviour doth plainly witness, that there shall not be as much as a cup of cold water bestowed for his sake without reward [Matthew x.42].

Hereupon dependeth whatsoever difference there is between the states of saints in glory; hither we refer whatsoever belongeth unto the highest perfection of man by way of service towards God; hereunto that fervour and first love of Christians did bend itself, causing them to sell their possessions, and lay down the price at the blessed Apostles' feet [Acts iv.34-35]. Hereat St. Paul undoubtedly did aim in so far abridging his own liberty, and exceeding that which the bond of necessary and enjoined duty tied him unto [1 Thess. ii.7, 9].

[5] Wherefore seeing that in all these several kinds of actions there can be nothing possibly evil which God approveth; and that he approveth much more than he doth command; and that his very commandments in some kind, as namely his precepts comprehended in the law of nature, may be otherwise known than only by Scripture; and that to do them, howsoever we know them, must needs be acceptable in his sight: let them with whom we have hitherto disputed consider well, how it can stand with reason to make the bare mandate of sacred Scripture the only rule of all good and evil in the actions of mortal men. The testimonies of God are true, the testimonies of God are perfect, the testimonies of God are all sufficient unto that end for which they were given. Therefore accordingly we do receive them, we do not think that in them God hath omitted any thing needful unto his purpose, and left his intent to be accomplished by our devisings. What the Scripture purposeth, the same in all points it doth perform.

Howbeit that here we swerve not in judgment, one thing especially we must observe, namely that the absolute perfection of Scripture is seen by relation unto that end whereto it tendeth. And even hereby it cometh to pass, that first such as imagine the general and main drift of the body of sacred Scripture not be so large as it is, nor that God did thereby intend to deliver, as in truth he doth, a full instruction in all things unto salvation necessary, the knowledge whereof man by nature could not otherwise in this life attain unto: they are by this very mean induced either still to look for new revelations from heaven, or else dangerously to add to the word of God uncertain tradition, that so the doctrine of man's salvation may be complete; which doctrine, we constantly hold in all respects without any such thing added to be so complete, that we utterly refuse as much as once to acquaint ourselves with any thing further. Whatsoever to make up the doctrine of man's salvation is added, as in supply of the Scripture's unsufficiency, we reject it. Scripture purposing this, hath perfectly and fully done it.

Again, the scope and purpose of God in delivering the Holy Scripture such as do take more largely than behoveth, they on the contrary side, racking and stretching it further than by him was meant, are drawn into sundry as great inconveniences. These pretending the Scripture's perfection infer thereupon, that in Scripture all things lawful to be done must needs be contained. We count those things perfect which want nothing requisite for the end whereto they were instituted. As therefore God created every part and particle of man exactly perfect, that is to say in all points sufficient unto that use for which he appointed it; so the Scripture, yea, every sentence thereof, is perfect, and wanteth nothing requisite unto that purpose for which God delivered the same. So that if hereupon we conclude, that because the Scripture is perfect, therefore all things lawful to be done are comprehended in the Scripture; we may even as well conclude so of every sentence, as of the whole sum and body thereof, unless we first of all prove that it was the drift, scope, and purpose of Almighty God in Holy Scripture to comprise all things which man may practise.

[6] But admit this, and mark, I beseech you, what would follow. God in delivering Scripture to his Church should clean have abrogated amongst them the law of nature; which is an infallible knowledge imprinted in the minds of all the chidren of men, whereby both general principles for directing of human actions are comprehended, and conclusions derived from them; upon which conclusions groweth in particularity the choice of good and evil in the daily affairs of this life. Admit this, and what shall the Scripture be but a snare and a torment to weak consciences, filling them with infinite perplexities, scrupulosities, doubts insoluble, and extreme despairs? Not that the Scripture itself doth

cause any such thing, (for it tendeth to the clean contrary, and the fruit thereof is resolute assurance and certainty in that it teacheth), but the necessities of this life urging men to do that which the light of nature, common discretion and judgment of itself directeth them unto; on the other side, this doctrine teaching them that so to do were to sin against their own souls, and that they put forth their hands to iniquity whatsoever they go about and have not first the sacred Scripture of God for direction; how can it choose but bring the simple a thousand times to their wits' end? how can it choose but vex and amaze them? For in every action of common life to find out some sentence clearly and infallibly setting before our eyes what we ought to do, (seem we in Scripture never so expert), would trouble us more than we are aware. In weak and tender minds we little know what misery this strict opinion would breed, besides the stops it would make in the whole course of all men's lives and actions. Make all things sin which we do by direction of nature's light, and by the rule of common discretion, without thinking at all upon Scripture; admit this position, and parents shall cause their children to sin, as oft as they cause them to do any thing, before they come to years of capacity and be ripe for knowledge in the Scripture: admit this, and it shall not be with masters as it was with him in the Gospel, but servants being commanded to go shall stand still, till they have their errand warranted unto them by Scripture [Luke vii.8]. Which as it standeth with Christian duty in some cases, so in common affairs to require it were most unfit.

[7] Two opinions therefore there are concerning sufficiency of Holy Scripture, each extremely opposite unto the other, and both repugnant unto truth. The schools of Rome teach Scripture to be so unsufficient, as if, except traditions were added, it did not contain all revealed and supernatural truth, which absolutely is necessary for the children of men in this life to know that they may in the next be saved. Others justly condemning this opinion grow likewise unto a dangerous extremity, as if Scripture did not only contain all things in that kind necessary, but all things simply, and in such sort that to do any thing according to any other law were not only unnecessary but even opposite unto salvation,

unlawful and sinful. Whatsoever is spoken of God or things appertaining to God otherwise than as the truth is, though it seem an honour it is an injury. And as incredible praises given unto men do often abate and impair the credit of their deserved commendation; so we must likewise take great heed, lest in attributing unto Scripture more than it can have, the incredibility of that do cause even those things which indeed it hath most abundantly to be less reverently esteemed. I therefore leave it to themselves to consider, whether they have in this first point or not overshot themselves; which God doth know is quickly done, even when our meaning is most sincere, as I am verily persuaded theirs in this case was.   (II.vii, viii)

Book III

Going on to deal with church order and government, Hooker distinguishes the invisible Church which is the mystical body of Christ and the visible Church on earth (24), and it is the latter with which he is concerned (III.i.14). He considers several Puritan views, again insisting on the necessary interconnection of reason and Scripture for the discovery of the truth (25), Scripture as first principles (26), reason enlightened by the Holy Spirit as interpreter (26). Doctrine is unchangeable, a matter of faith; order is not, a matter of regulation (27). Consistent with the predominantly pugnacious mood of this book, Hooker ends with a rigorous refutative conclusion (28).

24   THE NATURE OF THE CHURCH
AND ITS NEED OF A POLITY

I. Albeit the substance of those controversies whereinto we have begun to wade be rather of outward things appertaining to the Church of Christ, than of any thing wherein the nature and being of the Church consisteth, yet because the subject or matter which this position concerneth is, *A Form of Church Government* or *Church Polity*, it therefore behoveth us so far forth to consider the nature of the Church, as is requisite for men's more clear and plain understanding in what respect Laws of Polity or Government are necessary thereunto.

[2] That Church of Christ, which we properly term his body mystical, can be but one; neither can that one be sensibly discerned by any man, inasmuch as the parts thereof are some in heaven already with Christ, and the rest that are on earth (albeit their natural persons be visible) we do not discern under this property, whereby they are truly and infallibly of that body. Only our minds by intellectual conceit are able to apprehend, that such a real body there is, a body collective, because it containeth an huge multitude; a body mystical, because the mystery of their conjunction is removed altogether from sense. Whatsoever we read in Scripture concerning the endless love and the saving mercy which God sheweth towards his Church, the only proper

112

subject thereof is this Church. Concerning this flock it is that our Lord and Saviour hath promised, "I give unto them eternal life, and they shall never perish, neither shall any pluck them out of my hands" [John x.28]. They who are of this society have such marks and notes of distinction from all others, as are not object unto our sense; only unto God, who seeth their hearts and understandeth all their secret cogitations, unto him they are clear and manifest. All men knew Nathanael to be an Israelite. But our Saviour piercing deeper giveth further testimony of him than men could have done with such certainty as he did, "Behold indeed an Israelite in whom is no guile" [John i.47]. If we profess, as Peter did [John xxi.15], that we love the Lord, and profess it in the hearing of men, charity is prone to believe all things, and therefore charitable men are likely to think we do so, as long as they see no proof to the contrary. But that our love is sound and sincere, that it cometh from "a pure heart and a good conscience and a faith unfeigned" [1 Tim. i.5], who can pronounce, saving only the Searcher of all men's hearts, who alone intuitively doth know in this kind who are His?

[3] And as those everlasting promises of love, mercy, and blessedness belong to the mystical Church; even so on the other side when we read of any duty which the Church of God is bound unto, the Church whom this doth concern is a sensibly known company. And this visible Church in like sort is but one, continued from the first beginning of the world to the last end. Which company being divided into two moieties, the one before, the other since the coming of Christ; that part, which since the coming of Christ partly hath embraced and partly shall hereafter embrace the Christian religion, we term as by a more proper name the Church of Christ. And therefore the Apostle affirmeth plainly of all men Christian [1 Cor. xii.13], that be they Jews or Gentiles, bond or free, they are all incorporated into one company, they all make but *one body* [Eph. ii.16; iii.6]. The unity of which visible body and Church of Christ consisteth in that uniformity which all several persons thereunto belonging have, by reason of that *one Lord* whose servants they all profess themselves, that *one Faith* which they all acknowledge, that *one Baptism* wherewith they are all initiated [Eph. iv.5].

[4] The visible Church of Jesus Christ is therefore one, in outward profession of all those things, which supernaturally appertain to the very essence of Christianity, and are necessarily required in every particular Christian man. "Let all the house of Israel know for certainty", saith Peter, "that God hath made him both Lord and Christ, even this Jesus whom you have crucified" [Acts ii.36]. Christians therefore they are not, which call not him their Master and Lord [John xiii.13; Col. iii.24; iv.1]. And from hence it came that first at Antioch, and afterwards throughout the whole world, all that are of the Church visible were called Christians even amongst the heathen. Which name unto them was precious and glorious, but in the estimation of the rest of the world even Christ Jesus himself was execrable [1 Cor. i.23];[1] for whose sake all men were so likewise which did acknowledge him to be their Lord. This himself did foresee, and therefore armed his Church, to the end they might sustain it without discomfort. "All these things they will do unto you for my name's sake; yea, the time shall come, that whosoever killeth you will think that he doth God good service". "These things I tell you, that when the hour shall come, ye may then call to mind how I told you beforehand of them" [John xvi.2; 4].

[5] But our naming of Jesus Christ the Lord is not enough to prove us Christians, unless we also embrace that faith, which Christ hath published unto the world. To shew that the angel of Pergamus continued in Christianity, behold how the Spirit of Christ speaketh, "Thou keepest my name, and thou hast not denied my faith" [Rev. ii.13]. Concerning which faith, "the rule thereof", saith Tertullian, "is one alone, immovable, and no way possible to be better framed anew".[2] What rule that is he sheweth by rehearsing those few articles of Christian belief. And before Tertullian, Ireney; "The Church though scattered through the whole world unto the utmost borders of the earth, hath from the Apostles and their disciples received belief".[3] The parts of which belief he also

---

1 Tacitus, *Annals*, XV.44.
2 Tertullian, *De Virginibus*, c.1.
3 Irenaeus, *Adversum Haereses*, I.2 and 3.

reciteth, in substance the very same with Tertullian, and thereupon inferreth, "This faith the Church being spread far and wide preserveth as if one house did contain them: these things it equally embraceth, as though it had even one soul, one heart, and no more: it publisheth, teacheth and delivereth these things with uniform consent, as if God had given it but one only tongue wherewith to speak. He which amongst the guides of the Church is best able to speak uttereth no more than this, and less than this the most simple doth not utter", when they make profession of their faith.

[6] Now although we know the Christian faith and allow of it, yet in this respect we are but entering; entered we are not into the visible Church before our admittance by the door of Baptism. Wherefore immediately upon the acknowledgement of Christian faith, the Eunuch (we see) was baptized by Philip [Acts viii.38], Paul by Ananias [Acts xxii.16], by Peter an huge multitude containing three thousand souls [Acts ii.41], which being once baptized were reckoned in the number of souls added to the visible Church....

[14] By the Church therefore in this question we understand no other than only the visible Church. For preservation of Christianity there is not any thing more needful, than that such as are of the visible Church have mutual fellowship and society one with another. In which consideration, as the main body of the sea being one, yet within divers precincts hath divers names; so the Catholic Church is in like sort divided into a number of distinct Societies, every of which is termed a Church within itself. In this sense the Church is always a visible society of men; not an assembly, but a society. For although the name of the Church be given unto Christian assemblies, although any multitude of Christian men congregated may be termed by the name of a Church, yet assemblies properly are rather things that belong to a Church. Men are assembled for performance of public actions; which actions being ended, the assembly dissolveth itself and is no longer in being, whereas the Church which was assembled doth no less continue afterwards than before. "Where but three are, and they of the laity also (saith Tertullian), yet there is a Church".[1]

1   Tertullian, *Exhortatio ad Castitiam*, c.7.

that is to say, a Christian assembly. But a Church, as now we are to understand it, is a Society; that is, a number of men belonging unto some Christian fellowship, the place and limits whereof are certain. That wherein they have communion is the public exercise of such duties as those mentioned in the Apostles' Acts, *Instruction, Breaking of Bread*, and *Prayers* [Acts ii.42]. As therefore they that are of the mystical body of Christ have those inward graces and virtues, whereby they differ from all others, which are not of the same body; again, whosoever appertain to the visible body of the Church, they have also the notes of external profession, whereby the world knoweth what they are: after the same manner even the several societies of Christian men, unto every of which the name of a Church is given with addition betokening severalty, as the Church of Rome, Corinth, Ephesus, England, and so the rest, must be endued with correspondent general properties belonging unto them as they are public Christian societies. And of such properties common unto all societies Christian, it may not be denied that one of the very chiefest is Ecclesiastical Polity.

Which word I therefore the rather use, because the name of Government, as commonly men understand it in ordinary speech, doth not comprise the largeness of that whereunto in this question it is applied. For when we speak of Government, what doth the greatest part conceive thereby, but only the exercise of superiority peculiar unto rulers and guides of others? To our purpose therefore the name of Church-Polity will better serve, because it containeth both government and also whatsoever besides belongeth to the ordering of the Church in public. Neither is any thing in this degree more necessary than Church-Polity, which is a form of ordering the public spiritual affairs of the Church of God.   (III.i.1-6)

25   THE WORD OF GOD AND REASON

... A number there are, who think they cannot admire as they

ought the power and authority of the word of God, if in things
divine they should attribute any force to man's reason. For which
cause they never use reason so willingly as to disgrace reason. . . .

. . . [10] Unto the word of God, being in respect of that end for
which God ordained it perfect, exact, and absolute in itself, we
do not add reason as a supplement of any maim or defect therein,
but as a necessary instrument, without which we could not reap
by the Scripture's perfection that fruit and benefit which it yieldeth. . . .   (III.viii.4, 10)

26   SCRIPTURE, REASON AND THE HOLY SPIRIT

[13] Because we maintain that in Scripture we are taught all
things necessary unto salvation; hereupon very childishly it is by
some demanded, what Scripture can teach us the sacred authority
of the Scripture, upon the knowledge whereof our whole faith
and salvation dependeth? As though there were any kind of
science in the world which leadeth men into knowledge without
presupposing a number of things already known. No science doth
make known the first principles whereon it buildeth, but they
are always either taken as plain and manifest in themselves, or
as proved and granted already, some former knowledge having
made them evident. Scripture teacheth all supernatural revealed
truth, without the knowledge whereof salvation cannot be attained.
The main principle whereupon our belief of all things therein
contained dependeth, is, that the Scriptures are the oracles of
God himself. This in itself we cannot say is evident. For then all
men that hear it would acknowledge it in heart, as they do when
they hear that "every whole is more than any part of that whole",
because this in itself is evident. The other we know that all do
not acknowledge when they hear it. There must be therefore
some former knowledge presupposed which doth herein assure
the hearts of all believers. Scripture teacheth us that saving truth
which God hath discovered unto the world by revelation, and it
presumeth us taught otherwise that itself is divine and sacred.

[14] The question then being by what means we are taught this; some answer that to learn it we have no other way than only tradition; as namely that so we believe because both we from our predecessors and they from theirs have so received. But is this enough? That which all men's experience teacheth them may not in any wise be denied. And by experience we all know, that the first outward motive leading men so to esteem of the Scripture is the authority of God's Church. For when we know the whole Church of God hath that opinion of the Scripture, we judge it even at the first an impudent thing for any man bred and brought up in the Church to be of a contrary mind without cause. Afterwards the more we bestow our labour in reading or hearing the mysteries thereof, the more we find that the thing itself doth answer our received opinion concerning it. So that the former inducement prevailing somewhat with us before, doth now much more prevail, when the very thing hath ministered farther reason. If infidels or atheists chance at any time to call it in question, this giveth us occasion to sift what reason there is, whereby the testimony of the Church concerning Scripture, and our own persuasion which Scripture itself hath confirmed, may be proved a truth infallible. In which case the ancient Fathers being often constrained to shew, what warrant they had so much to rely upon the Scriptures, endeavoured still to maintain the authority of the books of God by arguments such as unbelievers themselves must needs think reasonable, if they judged thereof as they should. Neither is it a thing impossible or greatly hard, even by such kind of proofs so to manifest and clear that point, that no man living shall be able to deny it, without denying some apparent principle such as all men acknowledge to be true.

Wherefore if I believe the Gospel, yet is reason of singular use, for that it confirmeth me in this my belief the more: if I do not as yet believe, nevertheless to bring me to the number of believers except reason did somewhat help, and were an instrument which God doth use unto such purposes, what should it boot to dispute with infidels or godless persons for their conversion and persuasion in that point?

[15] Neither can I think that when grave and learned men do

sometime hold, that of this principle there is no proof but by the testimony of the Spirit, which assureth our hearts therein, it is their meaning to exclude utterly all force which any kind of reason may have in that behalf; but I rather incline to interpret such their speeches, as if they had more expressly set down, that other motives and inducements, be they never so strong and consonant unto reason, are notwithstanding uneffectual of themselves to work faith concerning this principle, if the special grace of the Holy Ghost concur not to the enlightening of our minds. For otherwise I doubt not but men of wisdom and judgment will grant, that the Church, in this point especially, is furnished with reason, to stop the mouths of her impious adversaries; and that as it were altogether bootless to allege against them what the Spirit hath taught us, so likewise that even to our ownselves it needeth caution and explication how the testimony of the Spirit may be discerned, by what means it may be known; lest men think that the Spirit of God doth testify those things which the Spirit of error suggesteth. The operations of the Spirit, especially these ordinary which be common unto all true Christian men, are as we know things secret and undiscernible even to the very soul where they are, because their nature is of another and an higher kind than that they can be by us perceived in this life. Wherefore albeit the Spirit lead us into all truth and direct us in all goodness, yet because these workings of the Spirit in us are so privy and secret, we therefore stand on a plainer ground, when we gather by reason from the quality of things believed or done, that the Spirit of God hath directed us in both, than if we settle ourselves to believe or to do any certain particular thing, as being moved thereto by the Spirit. (III.viii.13-15)

27   DOCTRINE UNCHANGEABLE, ACTION NOT

[7] Touching points of doctrine, as for example, the Unity of God, the Trinity of Persons, salvation by Christ, the resurrection of the body, life everlasting, the judgment to come, and such like,

they have been since the first hour that there was a Church in the world, and till the last they must be believed. But as for matters of regiment, they are for the most part of another nature. To make new articles of faith and doctrine no man thinketh it lawful; new laws of government what commonwealth or church is there which maketh not either at one time or another? "The rule of faith", saith Tertullian, "is but one, and that alone immoveable and impossible to be framed or cast anew".[1] The law of outward order and polity not so. There is no reason in the world wherefore we should esteem it as necessary always to do, as always to believe, the same things; seeing every man knoweth that the matter of faith is constant, the matter contrariwise of action daily changeable, especially the matter of action belonging unto church polity. (III.x.7)

28   CONCLUDING REFUTATION OF THE PURITANS

[21] As for those marvellous discourses whereby they adventure to argue that God must needs have done the thing which they imagine was to be done; I must confess I have often wondered at their exceeding boldness herein. When the question is whether God have delivered in Scripture (as they affirm he hath) a complete, particular, immutable form of church polity, why take they that other both presumptuous and superfluous labour to prove he should have done it; there being no way in this case to prove the deed of God, saving only by producing that evidence wherein he hath done it? But if there be no such thing apparent upon record, they do as if one should demand a legacy by force and virtue of some written testament, wherein there being no such thing specified, he pleadeth that there it must needs be, and bringeth arguments from the love or goodwill which always the testator bore him; imagining, that these or the like proofs will convict a testament to have that in it which other men can no

1   Tertullian, *De Virginibus*, c.1.

where by reading find. In matters which concern the actions of God, the most dutiful way on our part is to search what God hath done, and with meekness to admire that, rather than to dispute what he in congruity of reason ought to do. The ways which he hath whereby to do all things for the greatest good of his Church are moe in number than we can search, other in nature than that we should presume to determine which of many should be the fittest for him to choose, till such time as we see he hath chosen of many some one; which one we then may boldly conclude to be the fittest, because he hath taken it before the rest. When we do otherwise, surely we exceed our bounds; who and where we are we forget; and therefore needful it is that our pride in such cases be controlled, and our disputes beaten back with those demands of the blessed Apostle, "How unsearchable are his judgments, and his ways past finding out! Who hath known the mind of the Lord, or who was his counsellor?" [Romans xi.33-34]

(III.xi.21)

Book IV

In considering accusations of residual Romanism within the Church
of England (IV) Hooker deals first with the purpose and value of
ceremonies (29). He argues the impossibility, in what is a different
set of historical circumstances, of observing apostolic practice to the
letter, this latter in any case not comprehensively spelt out in Scripture (30). The so-called Romish ceremonies in the Church of England, he claims, are in fact not just Romish but part of "the ancient
rites and customs of the Church of Christ" (32). He pleads therefore
for a characteristic Anglican *via media* – to reform but not to overthrow (31, 33).

29   THE PURPOSE OF CEREMONIES

[3] The end which is aimed at in setting down the outward
form of all religious actions is the edification of the Church. Now
men are edified, when either their understanding is taught somewhat whereof in such actions it behoveth all men to consider, or
when their hearts are moved with any affection suitable thereunto; when their minds are in any sort stirred up into that reverence, devotion, attention, and due regard, which in those cases
seemeth requisite. Because therefore unto this purpose not only
speech but sundry sensible means besides have always been
thought necessary, and especially those means which being
object to the eye, the liveliest and the most apprehensive sense
of all other, have in that respect seemed the fittest to make a deep
and a strong impression: from hence have risen not only a number
of prayers, readings, questionings, exhortings, but even of visible
signs also; which being used in performance of holy actions, are
undoubtedly most effectual to open such matter, as men when
they know and remember carefully, must needs be a great deal
the better informed to what effect such duties serve. We must
not think but that there is some ground of reason even in nature,
whereby it cometh to pass that no nation under heaven either
doth or ever did suffer public actions which are of weight,
whether they be civil and temporal or else spiritual and sacred,

to pass without some visible solemnity: the very strangeness whereof and difference from that which is common, doth cause popular eyes to observe and to mark the same. Words, both because they are common, and do not so strongly move the fancy of man, are for the most part but slightly heard: and therefore with singular wisdom it hath been provided, that the deeds of men which are made in the presence of witnesses should pass not only with words, but also with certain sensible actions, the memory whereof is far more easy and durable than the memory of speech can be.

The things which so long experience of all ages hath confirmed and made profitable, let not us presume to condemn as follies and toys, because we sometimes know not the cause and reason of them.   (IV.i.3)

30   PRACTICE CHANGES WITH TIME

[3] Our end ought always to be the same; our ways and means thereunto not so. The glory of God and the good of His Church was the thing which the Apostles aimed at, and therefore ought to be the mark whereat we also level. But seeing those rites and orders may be at one time more which at another are less available unto that purpose, what reason is there in these things to urge the state of one only age as a pattern for all to follow? It is not I am right sure their meaning, that we should now assemble our people to serve God in close and secret meetings; or that common brooks or rivers should be used for places of baptism; or that the Eucharist should be ministered after meat; or that the custom of church feasting should be renewed; or that all kind of standing provision for the ministry should be utterly taken away, and their estate made again dependent upon the voluntary devotion of men. In these things they easily perceive how unfit that were for the present, which was for the first age convenient enough. The faith, zeal, and godliness of former times is worthily had in honour; but doth this prove that the orders of the Church of Christ

must be still the selfsame with theirs, that nothing may be which was not then, or that nothing which then was may lawfully since have ceased? They who recall the Church unto that which was at the first, must necessarily set bounds and limits unto their speeches. If any thing have been received repugnant unto that which was first delivered, the first things in this case must stand, the last give place unto them. But where difference is without repugnancy, that which hath been can be no prejudice to that which is. (IV.ii.3)

31   NEED FOR MODERATION IN PROCESS OF CHANGE

... We are contrariwise of opinion, that he which will perfectly recover a sick and restore a diseased body unto health, must not endeavour so much to bring it to a state of simple contrariety, as of fit proportion in contrariety unto those evils which are to be cured. He that will take away extreme heat by setting the body in extremity of cold, shall undoubtedly remove the disease, but together with it the diseased too. The first thing therefore in skilful cures is the knowledge of the part affected; the next is of the evil which doth affect it; the last is not only of the kind but also of the measure of contrary things whereby to remove it.

(IV.viii.1)

32   ANGLICAN RITES COMMON WITH ROME
REALLY ANCIENT CHRISTIAN RITES

IX. That the church of Rome doth hereby take occasion to blaspheme, and to say, our religion is not able to stand of itself unless it lean upon the staff of their ceremonies, is not a matter of so great moment, that it did need to be objected, or doth deserve to receive an answer. The name of blasphemy in this place, is like the shoe of Hercules on a child's foot. If the church of Rome

do use any such kind of silly exprobration, it is no such ugly
thing to the ear, that we should think the honour and credit of
our religion to receive thereby any great wound. They which
hereof make so perilous a matter do seem to imagine, that we
have erected of late a frame of some new religion, the furniture
whereof we should not have borrowed from our enemies, lest
they relieving us might afterwards laugh and gibe at our poverty;
whereas in truth the ceremonies which we have taken from such
as were before us, are not things that belong to this or that sect,
but they are the ancient rites and customs of the Church of Christ,
whereof ourselves being a part, we have the selfsame interest in
them which our fathers before us had, from whom the same are
descended unto us.   (IV.ix.1)

33   GRADUAL REFORM FAVOURED
BY CHURCH OF ENGLAND

. . . The church of England being to alter her received laws concerning such orders, rites, and ceremonies, as had been in former
times an hinderance unto piety and religious service of God, was
to enter into consideration first, that the change of laws, especially
concerning matter of religion, must be warily proceeded in. Laws,
as all other things human, are many times full of imperfection;
and that which is supposed behoveful unto men, proveth oftentimes most pernicious. The wisdom which is learned by tract of
time, findeth the laws that have been in former ages established,
needful in later to be abrogated. Besides, that which sometime
is expedient doth not always so continue: and the number of
needless laws unabolished doth weaken the force of them that
are necessary. But true withal it is, that alteration though it be
from worse to better hath in it inconveniences, and those weighty;
unless it be in such laws as have been made upon special
occasions, which occasions ceasing, laws of that kind do abrogate
themselves. But when we abrogate a law as being ill made, the
whole cause for which it was made still remaining, do we not

herein revoke our very own deed, and upbraid ourselves with
folly, yea, all that were makers of it with oversight and with
error? Further, if it be a law which the custom and continual
practice of many ages or years hath confirmed in the minds of
men, to alter it must needs be troublesome and scandalous. It
amazeth them, it causeth them to stand in doubt whether any
thing be in itself by nature either good or evil, and not all things
rather such as men at this or that time agree to account of them,
when they behold even those things disproved, disannulled,
rejected, which use had made in a manner natural. What have
we to induce men unto the willing obedience and observation of
laws, but the weight of so many men's judgment as have with
deliberate advice assented thereunto; the weight of that long
experience, which the world hath had thereof with consent and
good liking? So that to change any such law must needs with the
common sort impair and weaken the force of those grounds,
whereby all laws are made effectual.

[2] Notwithstanding we do not deny alteration of laws to be
sometimes a thing necessary; as when they are unnatural, or
impious, or otherwise hurtful unto the public community of men,
and against that good for which human societies were instituted.
... As for arbitrary alterations, when laws in themselves not simply bad or unmeet are changed for better and more expedient; if
the benefit of that which is newly better devised be but small,
sith the custom of easiness to alter and change is so evil, no doubt
but to bear a tolerable sore is better than to venture on a dangerous
remedy.

[3] Which being generally thought upon as a matter that
touched nearly their whole enterprise, whereas change was notwithstanding concluded necessary, in regard of the great hurt
which the Church did receive by a number of things then in use,
whereupon a great deal of that which had been was now to be
taken away and removed out of the Church; yet sith there are
divers ways of abrogating things established, they saw it best to
cut off presently such things as might in that sort be extinguished
without danger, leaving the rest to be abolished by disusage
through tract of time....   (IX.xiv.1-3)

Book V

Hooker is now ready to move on to his great *apologia* for Anglicanism, the wonderful Fifth Book. Typically, he begins with fundamentals: the relationship of the spiritual and the temporal, of religion with justice and benevolence (34) and the importance of religion as against atheism and superstition. He then puts four propositions about rites and customs in worship, viz. (a) the need for intrinsic reasonableness (35), (b) the worth of ancient precept and practice (35), (c) the authority of the Church (35) and (d) the need to allow for change (35). As against these, private judgments cannot be considered as a safe criterion (V.x.1).

Thereafter Hooker considers the several aspects of Anglican practice: church buildings (V.xi-xvii), the reading of lessons *vis-à-vis* Puritan exaltation of preaching (V.xviii-xxli as, for example, in 36 and 37), prayer and the liturgy (37, 38), psalms and canticles, and other elements of the Anglican services (42, 43), the Sacraments and their relation to the Incarnation (44-47), baptism (48-52), the Eucharist (53-55), followed by miscellanea on the occasional services.

What Hooker has to say on prayer and the sacraments shows him at his best. The eloquence of his eulogy on prayer in general (37) is followed by a balanced appreciation of public prayer and the Anglican liturgy (38). This is matched by his words on the sacraments (44) and on the Incarnation (45) which is central for Hooker in any real understanding of the sacraments (46), leading to his grand statement of their necessity for the Christian's participation in Christ (47). Seeing a triple significance in the sacraments (48), he then goes on to consider baptism (49) and the Eucharist (47) separately. The book ends with a lofty estimate of the ministerial vocation (55).

It is worth mentioning that at several points Hooker rightly identifies and separates the important and the less so – for example, the fuss about the minister's position at various times of the service (41) as against the value of the cross in baptism (52), the inadmissibility of female ministry (50) and the wholly unacceptable refusal of baptism where the sponsors are not evidently believers (51). Once again (in his section on crossing in baptism) Hooker sensibly opts for the middle way (54).

34   TRUE RELIGION AND SOCIAL ORDER

I. Few there are of so weak capacity, but public evils they easily espy; fewer so patient, as not to complain, when the grievous inconveniences thereof work sensible smart. Howbeit to see wherein the harm which they feel consisteth, the seeds from which it sprang, and the method of curing it, belongeth to a skill, the study whereof is so full of toil, and the practice so beset with difficulties, that wary and respective men had rather seek quietly their own, and wish that the world may go well, so it be not long of them, than with pain and hazard make themselves advisers for the common good. We which thought it at the very first a sign of cold affection towards the Church of God, to prefer private ease before the labour of appeasing public disturbance, must now of necessity refer events to the gracious providence of Almighty God, and, in discharge of our duty towards him, proceed with the plain and unpartial defence of a common cause. Wherein our endeavour is not so much to overthrow them with whom we contend, as to yield them just and reasonable causes of those things, which, for want of due consideration heretofore, they misconceived, accusing laws for men's oversights, imputing evils, grown through personal defects unto that which is not evil, framing unto some sores unwholesome plaisters, and applying other some where no sore is.

[2] To make therefore our beginning that which to both parts is most acceptable, We agree that pure and unstained religion ought to be the highest of all cares appertaining to public regiment: as well in regard of that aid and protection [Psalm cxliv.2] which they who faithfully serve God confess they receive at his merciful hands; as also for the force which religion hath to qualify all sorts of men, and to make them in public affairs the more serviceable, governors the apter to rule with conscience, inferiors for conscience' sake the willinger to obey. It is no peculiar conceit, but a matter of sound consequence, that all duties are by so much the better performed, by how much the men are more religious from whose abilities the same proceed. For if the course of politic affairs cannot in any good sort go forward without fit instruments,

and that which fitteth them be their virtues, let Polity acknowledge itself indebted to Religion; godliness being the chiefest top and wellspring of all true virtues, even as God is of all good things.

So natural is the union of Religion with Justice, that we may boldly deem there is neither, where both are not. For how should they be unfeignedly just, whom religion doth not cause to be such; or they religious, which are not found such by the proof of their just actions? If they, which employ their labour and travail about the public administration of justice, follow it only as a trade, with unquenchable and unconscionable thirst of gain, being not in heart persuaded that justice is God's own work, and themselves his agents in this business, the sentence of right God's own verdict, and themselves his priests to deliver it; formalities of justice do but serve to smother right, and that, which was necessarily ordained for the common good, is through shameful abuse made the cause of common misery.

The same piety, which maketh them that are in authority desirous to please and resemble God by justice, inflameth every way men of action with zeal to do good (as far as their place will permit) unto all. For that, they know, is most noble and divine. Whereby if no natural nor casual inability cross their desires, they always delighting to inure themselves with actions most beneficial to others, cannot but gather great experience, and through experience the more wisdom; because conscience, and the fear of swerving from that which is right, maketh them diligent observers of circumstances, the loose regard whereof is the nurse of vulgar folly, no less than Salomon's attention thereunto was of natural furtherances the most effectual to make him eminent above others. For he gave good heed, and pierced every thing to the very ground, and by that mean became the author of many parables [Eccles. xii.9-10].   (V.i.1-2)

35   TESTS OF CHURCH ORDER

(i) Intrinsic Reasonableness

VI. The first thing therefore which is of force to cause approbation with good conscience towards such customs or rites as publicly are established, is when there riseth from the due consideration of those customs and rites in themselves apparent reason, although not always to prove them better than any other that might possibly be devised, (for who did ever require this in man's ordinances?) yet competent to shew their conveniency and fitness, in regard of the use for which they should serve.

Now touching the nature of religious services, and the manner of their due performance, thus much generally we know to be most clear; that whereas the greatness and dignity of all manner actions is measured by the worthiness of the subject from which they proceed, and of the object whereabout they are conversant, we must of necessity in both respects acknowledge, that this present world affordeth not any thing comparable unto the public duties of religion. For if the best things have the perfectest and best operations, it will follow, that seeing man is the worthiest creature upon earth, and every society of men more worthy than any man, and of societies that most excellent which we call the Church; there can be in this world no work performed equal to the exercise of true religion, the proper operation of the Church of God.

Again, forasmuch as religion worketh upon him who in majesty and power is infinite, as we ought we account not of it, unless we esteem it even according to that very height of excellency which our hearts conceive when divine sublimity itself is rightly considered. In the powers and faculties of our souls God requireth the uttermost which our unfeigned affection towards him is able to yield [John iv.24; 1 Chr. xxix.17]. So that if we affect him not far above and before all things, our religion hath not that inward perfection which it should have, neither do we indeed worship him as our God.

[2] That which inwardly each man should be, the Church out-

wardly ought to testify. And therefore the duties of our religion
which are seen must be such as that affection which is unseen
ought to be. Signs must resemble the things they signify. If religion bear the greatest sway in our hearts, our outward religious
duties must shew it as far as the Church hath outward ability.
Duties of religion performed by whole societies of men, ought
to have in them according to our power a sensible excellency,
correspondent to the majesty of him whom we worship [2 Chr.
ii.5]. Yea then are the public duties of religion best ordered, when
the militant Church doth resemble by sensible means, as it may
in such cases, that hidden dignity and glory wherewith the
Church triumphant in heaven is beautified.

Howbeit, even as the very heat of the sun itself, which is the
life of the whole world, was to the people of God in the desert
a grievous annoyance, for ease whereof his extraordinary providence ordained a cloudy pillar to overshadow them: so things of
general use and benefit (for in this world what is so perfect that
no inconvenience doth ever follow it?) may by some accident be
incommodious to a few. In which case, for such private evils
remedies there are of like condition, though public ordinances,
wherein the common good is respected, be not stirred.

Let our first demand be therefore, that in the external form of
religion such things as are apparently, or can be sufficiently
proved, effectual and generally fit to set forward godliness, either
as betokening the greatness of God, or as beseeming the dignity
of religion, or as concurring with celestial impressions in the
minds of men, may be reverently thought of; some few, rare,
casual, and tolerable, or otherwise curable inconveniences notwithstanding.   (V.vi)

(ii) The Argument from Antiquity

VII. Neither may we in this case lightly esteem what hath been
allowed as fit in the judgment of antiquity, and by the long continued practice of the whole Church; from which unnecessarily
to swerve, experience hath never as yet found it safe. For wisdom's

sake we reverence them no less that are young, or not much less, than if they were stricken in years. And therefore of such it is rightly said that their ripeness of understanding is "grey hair", and their virtues "old age" [Wisdom iv.9]. But because wisdom and youth are seldom joined in one, and the ordinary course of the world is more according to Job's observation, who giveth men advice to seek "wisdom amongst the ancient, and in the length of days, understanding" [Job xii.12]; therefore if the comparison do stand between man and man, which shall hearken unto other; sith the aged for the most part are best experienced, least subject to rash and unadvised passions, it hath been ever judged reasonable that their sentence in matter of counsel should be better trusted, and more relied upon than other men's. The goodness of God having furnished man with two chief instruments both necessary for this life, hands to execute and a mind to devise great things; the one is not profitable longer than the vigour of youth doth strengthen it, nor the other greatly till age and experience have brought it to perfection. In whom therefore time hath not perfected knowledge, such must be contented to follow them in whom it hath. For this cause none is more attentively heard than they whose speeches are as David's were, "I have been young and now am old" [Psalm xxxvii.25], much I have seen and observed in the world. Sharp and subtile discourses of wit procure many times very great applause, but being laid in the balance with that which the habit of sound experience plainly delivereth, they are overweighed. God may endue men extraordinarily with understanding as it pleaseth him. But let no man presuming thereupon neglect the instructions, or despise the ordinances of his elders, sith He whose gift wisdom is hath said, "Ask thy father and he will shew thee; thine ancients and they shall tell thee" [Deut. xxxii.7].

[2] It is therefore the voice both of God and nature, not of learning only, that especially in matters of action and policy, "The sentences and judgments of men experienced, aged and wise, yea though they speak without any proof or demonstration, are no less to be hearkened unto, than as being demonstrations in themselves; because such men's long observation is as an eye,

wherewith they presently and plainly behold those principles which sway over all actions".[1] Whereby we are taught both the cause wherefore wise men's judgments should be credited, and the mean how to use their judgments to the increase of our own wisdom. That which sheweth them to be wise, is the gathering of principles out of their own particular experiments. And the framing of our particular experiments according to the rule of their principles shall make us such as they are.

[3] If therefore even at the first so great account should be made of wise men's counsels touching things that are publicly done as time shall add thereunto continuance and approbation of succeeding ages, their credit and authority must needs be greater. They which do nothing but that which men of account did before them, are, although they do amiss, yet the less faulty, because they are not the authors of harm. And doing well, their actions are freed from prejudice of novelty. To the best and wisest, while they live, the world is continually a froward opposite, a curious observer of their defects and imperfections; their virtues it afterwards as much admireth. And for this cause many times that which most deserveth approbation would hardly be able to find favour, if they which propose it were not content to profess themselves therein scholars and followers of the ancient. For the world will not endure to hear that we are wiser than any have been which went before. In which consideration there is cause why we should be slow and unwilling to change, without very urgent necessity, the ancient ordinances, rites, and long approved customs, of our venerable predecessors. The love of things ancient doth argue stayedness, but levity and want of experience maketh apt unto innovations. That which wisdom did first begin, and hath been with good men long continued, challengeth allowance of them that succeed, although it plead for itself nothing. That which is new, if it promise not much, doth fear condemnation before trial; till trial, no man doth acquit or trust it, what good soever it pretend and promise. So that in this kind there are few things known to be good, till such time as they grow to be ancient.

1 Aristotle, *Ethics*, VI.11.

The vain pretence of those glorious names, where they could not
be with any truth, neither in reason ought to have been so much
alleged, hath wrought such a prejudice against them in the minds
of the common sort, as if they had utterly no force at all; whereas
(especially for these observances which concern our present question) antiquity, custom, and consent in the Church of God, making with that which law doth establish, are themselves most
sufficient reasons to uphold the same, unless some notable public
inconvenience enforce the contrary. For a small thing in the eye
of law is as nothing.[1]

[4] We are therefore bold to make our second petition this,
That in things the fitness whereof is not of itself apparent, nor
easy to be made sufficiently manifest unto all, yet the judgment
of antiquity concurring with that which is received may induce
them to think it not unfit, who are not able to allege any known
weighty inconvenience which it hath, or to take any strong exception against it.   (V.vii)

(iii) Church Authority

VIII. All things cannot be of ancient continuance, which are
expedient and needful for the ordering of spiritual affairs: but
the Church being a body which dieth not hath always power, as
occasion requireth, no less to ordain that which never was, than
to ratify what hath been before. To prescribe the order of doing
in all things, is a peculiar prerogative which Wisdom hath, as
queen or sovereign commandress over other virtues. This in
every several man's actions of common life appertaineth unto
Moral, in public and politic secular affairs unto Civil wisdom. In
like manner, to devise any certain form for the outward administration of public duties in the service of God, or things belonging
thereunto, and to find out the most convenient for that use, is a
point of wisdom Ecclesiastical.

[2] It is not for a man which doth know or should know what

1   Aristotle, *Ethics*, II.9.

order is, and what peaceable government requireth, to ask, "why we should hang our judgment upon the Church's sleeve"; and "why in matters of order, more than in matters of doctrine".[1] The Church hath authority to establish that for an order at one time, which at another time it may abolish, and in both do well. But that which in doctrine the Church doth now deliver rightly as a truth, no man will say that it may hereafter recall, and as rightly avouch the contrary. Laws touching matter of order are changeable, by the power of the Church; articles concerning doctrine not so. ....

[5] We therefore crave thirdly to have it granted, That where neither the evidence of any law divine, nor the strength of any invincible argument otherwise found out by the light of reason nor any notable public inconvenience, doth make against that which our own laws ecclesiastical have although but newly instituted for the ordering of these affairs, the very authority of the Church itself, at the least in such cases, may give so much credit to her own laws, as to make their sentence touching fitness and conveniency weightier than any bare and naked conceit to the contrary; especially in them who can owe no less than child-like obedience to her that hath more than motherly power.

(V. viii. 1, 2, 5)

(iv) Acceptance of Necessary Change

IX. There are ancient ordinances, laws which on all sides are allowed to be just and good, yea divine and apostolic constitutions, which the church it may be doth not always keep, nor always justly deserve blame in that respect. For in evils that cannot be removed without the manifest danger of greater to succeed in their rooms, wisdom, of necessity, must give place to necessity. ....

[5] These things therefore considered, we lastly require that it may not seem hard, if in cases of necessity, or for common utility's

1   Cartwright, III, p.171.

sake, certain profitable ordinances sometime be released rather than all men always strictly bound to the general rigour thereof.

(V.ix.1, 5)

36   THE PURPOSE OF THE WORD OF GOD

[3] The end of the word of God is *to save*, and therefore we term it *the word of life*. The way for all men to be saved is by the knowledge of that truth which the word hath taught. And sith eternal life is a thing of itself communicable unto all, it behoveth that the word of God, the necessary mean thereunto, be so likewise. Wherefore the word of life hath been always a treasure, though precious, yet easy, as well to attain, as to find; lest any man desirous of life should perish through the difficulty of the way. To this end the word of God no otherwise serve it than only in the nature of a doctrinal instrument. It saveth because it maketh "wise to salvation" [2 Tim. iii.15]. Wherefore the ignorant it saveth not; they which live by the word must know it. And being itself the instrument which God hath purposely framed, thereby to work the knowledge of salvation in the hearts of men, what cause is there wherefore it should not of itself be acknowledged a most apt and a likely mean to leave an Apprehension of things divine in our understanding, and in the mind an Assent thereunto? For touching the one, sith God, who knoweth and discloseth best the rich treasures of his own wisdom, hath by delivering his word made choice of the Scriptures as the most effectual means whereby those treasures might be imparted unto the world, it followeth that to man's understanding the Scripture must needs be even of itself intended as a full and perfect discovery, sufficient to imprint in us the lively character of all things necessarily required for the attainment of eternal life. And concerning our Assent to the mysteries of heavenly truth, seeing that the word of God for the Author's sake hath credit with all that confess it (as we all do) to be his word, every proposition of holy Scripture, every sentence being to us a principle; if the

principles of all kinds of knowledge else have that virtue in themselves, whereby they are able to procure our assent unto such
conclusions as the industry of right discourse doth gather from
them; we have no reason to think the principles of that truth
which tendeth unto man's everlasting happiness less forcible
than any other, when we know that of all other they are for their
certainty the most infallible. . . .

[2] Touching therefore the use of Scripture, even in that it is
openly read, and the inestimable good which the Church of God
by that very mean hath reaped; there was, we may very well
think, some cause, which moved the Apostle St. Paul to require,
that those things which any one church's affairs gave particular
occasion to write, might for the instruction of all be published,
and that by reading [1 Thess. v.27; Col. iv.16].

1. When the very having of the books of God was a matter of
no small charge and difficulty, inasmuch as they could not be
had otherwise than only in written copies, it was the necessity
not of preaching things agreeable with the word, but of reading
the word itself at large to the people, which caused churches
throughout the world to have public care, that the sacred oracles
of God being procured by common charge, might with great
sedulity be kept both entire and sincere. If then we admire the
providence of God in the same continuance of Scripture, notwithstanding the violent endeavours of infidels to abolish, and
the fraudulent of heretics always to deprave the same, shall we
set light by that custom of reading, from whence so precious a
benefit hath grown?

2. The voice and testimony of the Church acknowledging Scripture to be the law of the living God, is for the truth and certainty
thereof no mean evidence. For if with reason we may presume
upon things which a few men's depositions do testify, suppose
we that the minds of men are not both at their first access to the
school of Christ exceedingly moved, yea and for ever afterwards
also confirmed much, when they consider the main consent of
all the churches in the whole world witnessing the sacred authority of scriptures, ever sithence the first publication thereof, even
till this present day and hour? And that they all have always so

testified, I see not how we should possibly wish a proof more palpable, than this manifest received and every where continued custom of reading them publicly as the Scriptures. The reading therefore of the word of God, as the use hath ever been, in open audience, is the plainest evidence we have of the Church's Assent and Acknowledgment that it is his word.

3. A further commodity this custom hath, which is to furnish the very simplest and rudest sort with such infallible Axioms and Precepts of sacred truth, delivered even in the very Letter of the Law of God, as may serve them for Rules whereby to judge the better all *other doctrines* and instructions which they hear [John v.39; Isaiah viii.2].   (V.xxi.3, xxii.2)

37 PRAYER

XXIII. Between the throne of God in heaven and his Church upon earth here militant if it be so that Angels have their continual intercourse, where should we find the same more verified than in these two ghostly exercises, the one Doctrine, and the other Prayer? For what is the assembling of the Church to learn, but the receiving of Angels descended from above? What to pray, but the sending of Angels upward? His heavenly inspirations and our holy desires are as so many Angels of intercourse and commerce between God and us. As teaching bringeth us to know that God is our supreme truth; so prayer testifieth that we acknowledge him our sovereign good.

Besides, sith on God as the most high all inferior causes in the world are dependent; and the higher any cause is, the more it coveteth to impart virtue unto things beneath it; how should any kind of service we do or can do find greater acceptance than prayer, which sheweth our concurrence with him in desiring that wherewith his very nature doth most delight?

Is not the name of prayer usual to signify even all the service that ever we do unto God? And that for no other cause, as I suppose, but to shew that there is in religion no acceptable duty which devout invocation of the name of God doth not either presuppose or infer. Prayers are those "calves of men's lips" [Hosea xiv.2]; those most gracious and sweet odours [Rev. v.8]; those rich presents and gifts which, being carried up into heaven [Acts x.4], do best testify our dutiful affection, and are for the purchasing of all favour at the hands of God the most undoubted means we can use.

On others what more easily, and yet what more fruitfully bestowed than our prayers? If we give counsel, they are the simpler only that need it; if alms, the poorer only are relieved; but by prayer we do good to all. And whereas every other duty besides is but to shew itself as time and opportunity require, for this all times are convenient [Romans i.9; Luke xviii.1]: when we are not able to do any other thing for men's behoof, when through maliciousness or unkindness they vouchsafe not to accept any other good at our hands, prayer is that which we always have in our power to bestow, and they never in theirs to refuse. Wherefore "God forbid", saith Samuel, speaking unto a most unthankful people, a people weary of the benefit of his most virtuous government over them, "God forbid that I should sin against the Lord, and cease to pray for you" [1 Samuel xii.23]. It is the first thing wherewith a righteous life beginneth, and the last wherewith it doth end.

The knowledge is small which we have on earth concerning things that are done in heaven. Notwithstanding thus much we know even of Saints in heaven, that they pray [Rev. vi.9]. And therefore prayer being a work common to the Church as well triumphant as militant, a work common unto men with Angels, what should we think but that so much of our lives is celestial and divine as we spend in the exercise of prayer? For which cause we see that the most comfortable visitations, which God hath sent men from above, have taken especially the times of prayer as their most natural opportunities [Daniel ix.20; Acts x.30].

                                                                        (V.xxiii)

38   PUBLIC PRAYER

XXIV. This holy and religious duty of service towards God concerneth us one way in that we are men, and another way in that we are joined as parts to that visible mystical body which is his Church. As men, we are at our own choice, both for time, and place, and form, according to the exigence of our own occasions in private [Psalm lv.17; Daniel ix.3; Acts x.9]; but the service, which we do as members of a public body, is public, and for that cause must needs be accounted by so much worthier than the other, as a whole society of such condition exceedeth the worth of any one. In which consideration unto Christian assemblies there are most special promises made [Matthew xviii.20]. St. Paul, though likely to prevail with God as much as [any] one, did notwithstanding think it much more both for God's glory and his own good, if prayers might be made and thanks yielded in his behalf by a number of men [2 Cor. i.11]. The prince and people of Nineveh assembling themselves as a main army of supplicants, it was not in the power of God to withstand them [Jonah iv.11]. I speak no otherwise concerning the force of public prayer in the Church of God, than before me Tertullian hath done, "We come by troops to the place of assembly, that being banded as it were together, we may be supplicants enough to besiege God with our prayers. These forces are unto him acceptable".[1]

[2] When we publicly make our prayers, it cannot be but that we do it with much more comfort than in private, for that the things we ask publicly are approved as needful and good in the judgment of all, we hear them sought for and desired with common consent. Again, thus much help and furtherance is more yielded, in that if so be our zeal and devotion to Godward be slack, the alacrity and fervour of others serveth as a present spur [Psalm cxxii.1]. "For even prayer itself" (saith St. Basil) "when it hath not the consort of many voices to strengthen it, is not itself".[2]

1   Tertullian, *Apology*, c.39.
2   Basil, *Epistles*, 68.

Finally, the good which we do by public prayer is more than in private can be done, for that besides the benefit which here is no less procured to ourselves, the whole Church is much bettered by our good example; and consequently whereas secret neglect of our duty in this kind is but only our own hurt, one man's contempt of the common prayer of the Church of God may and oftentimes is most hurtful unto many. In which considerations the prophet David so often voweth unto God the sacrifice of praise and thanksgiving in the congregation [Psalm xxvi.12; xxxiv.1]; so earnestly exhorteth others to sing praises unto the Lord in his courts, in his sanctuary, before the memorial of his holiness [Psalm xxx.4; xcvi.9]; and so much complaineth of his own uncomfortable exile, wherein although he sustained many most grievous indignities, and endureth the want of sundry both pleasures and honours before enjoyed, yet as if this one were his only grief and the rest not felt, his speeches are all of the heavenly benefit of public assemblies, and the happiness of such as had free access thereunto [Psalm xxvii.4; xlii.4; lxxxiv.1].

XXV. A great part of the cause, wherefore religious minds are so inflamed with the love of public devotion, is that virtue, force, and efficacy, which by experience they find that the very form and reverend solemnity of common prayer duly ordered hath, to help that imbecility and weakness in us, by means whereof we are otherwise of ourselves the less apt to perform unto God so heavenly a service, with such affection of heart, and disposition in the powers of our souls as is requisite. To this end therefore all things hereunto appertaining have been ever thought convenient to be done with the most solemnity and majesty that the wisest could devise. It is not with public as with private prayer. In this rather secresy is commended than outward show [Matthew vi.5-6], whereas that being the public act of a whole society, requireth accordingly more care to be had of external appearance. The very assembling of men therefore unto this service hath been ever solemn.

[2] And concerning the place of assembly, although it serve for other uses as well as this, yet seeing that our Lord himself hath to this as to the chiefest of all other plainly sanctified his own

temple, by entitling it "the House of Prayer", what preeminence
of dignity soever hath been either by the ordinance or through
the special favour and providence of God annexed unto his
Sanctuary, the principal cause thereof must needs be in regard
of Common Prayer. For the honour and furtherance whereof, if
it be as the gravest of the ancient Fathers seriously were persuaded, and do oftentimes plainly teach, affirming that the house
of prayer is a Court beautified with the presence of celestial powers; that there we stand, we pray, we sound forth hymns unto
God, having his Angels intermingled as our associates; and that
with reference hereunto the Apostle doth require so great care
to be had of decency for the Angels' sake [1 Cor. xi.10]; how can
we come to the house of prayer, and not be moved with the very
glory of the place itself [Psalm xcvi.6], so to frame our affections
praying, as doth best beseem them, whose suits the Almighty
doth there sit to hear, and his Angels attend to further? When
this was ingrafted in the minds of men, there needed no penal
statutes to draw them unto public prayer. The warning sound
was no sooner heard, but the churches were presently filled, the
pavements covered with bodies prostrate, and washed with their
tears of devout joy.

[3] And as the place of public prayer is a circumstance in the
outward form thereof, which hath moment to help devotion; so
the person much more with whom the people of God do join
themselves in this action, as with him that standeth and speaketh
in the presence of God for them. The authority of his place, the
fervour of his zeal, the piety and gravity of his whole behaviour
must needs exceedingly both grace and set forward the service
he doth.

The Authority of his calling is a furtherance, because if God
have so far received him into favour, as to impose upon him by
the hands of men that office of blessing the people in his name,
and making intercession to him in theirs; which office he hath
sanctified with his own most gracious promise [Numbers vi.23],
and ratified that promise by manifest actual performance thereof,
when others before in like place have done the same [2 Chr.
xxx.27]; is not his very ordination a seal as it were to us, that the

selfsame divine love, which hath chosen the instrument to work with, will by that instrument effect the thing whereto he ordained it, in blessing his people and accepting the prayers which his servant offereth up unto God for them? It was in this respect a comfortable title which the ancient used to give unto God's ministers, terming them usually *God's most beloved*,[1] which were ordained to procure by their prayers his love and favour towards all.

Again, if there be not zeal and fervency in him which proposeth for the rest those suits and supplications which they by their joyful acclamations must ratify; if he praise not God with all his might; if he pour not out his soul in prayer; if he take not their causes to heart, or speak not as Moses, Daniel, and Ezra did for their people: how should there be but in them frozen coldness, when his affections seem benumbed from whom theirs should take fire.

Virtue and godliness of life are required at the hands of the minister of God, not only in that he is to teach and instruct the people, who for the most part are rather led away by the ill example, than directed aright by the wholesome instruction of them, whose life swerveth from the rule of their own doctrine; but also much more in regard of this other part of his function; whether we respect the weakness of the people, apt to loathe and abhor the sanctuary when they which perform the service thereof are such as the sons of Heli were [1 Samuel ii.12]; or else consider the inclination of God himself, who requireth the lifting up of pure hands in prayer [1 Tim. ii.8], and hath given the world plainly to understand that the wicked although they cry shall not be heard [John ix.31; Jer. xi.11; Ezek. viii.18]. They are no fit supplicants to seek his mercy in behalf of others, whose own unrepented sins provoke his just indignation. Let thy Priests therefore, O Lord, be evermore clothed with righteousness, that thy saints may thereby with more devotion rejoice and sing [Psalm cxxxii.9].

[4] But of all helps for due performance of this service the greatest is that very set and standing order itself, which framed with common advice, hath both for matter and form prescribed

1 For example Justinian, *Codex*, I.3.

whatsoever is herein publicly done. No doubt from God it hath proceeded, and by us it must be acknowledged a work of his singular care and providence, that the Church hath evermore held a prescript form of common prayer, although not in all things every where the same, yet for the most part retaining still the same analogy. So that if the liturgies of all ancient churches throughout the world be compared amongst themselves, it may be easily perceived they had all one original mould, and that the public prayers of the people of God in churches throughly settled did never use to be voluntary dictates proceeding from any man's extemporal wit.

[5] To him which considereth the grievous and scandalous inconveniences whereunto they make themselves daily subject, with whom any blind and secret corner is judged a fit house of common prayer; the manifold confusions which they fall into where every man's private spirit and gift (as they term it) is the only Bishop that ordaineth him to this ministry; the irksome deformities whereby through endless and senseless effusions of indigested prayers they oftentimes disgrace in most unsufferable manner the worthiest part of Christian duty towards God, who herein are subject to no certain order, but pray both what and how they list: to him I say which weigheth duly in all these things the reasons cannot be obscure, why God doth in public prayer so much respect the solemnity of places where [2 Chr. vi.20], the authority and calling of persons by whom [Joel iii.17], and the precise appointment even with what words or sentences his name should be called on amongst his people [2 Chr. xxix.30].

(V.xxiv, xxv)

39 ANGLICAN, ROMAN AND ANCIENT PRACTICE

XXVIII. Touching our conformity with the church of Rome, as also of the difference between some reformed churches and ours, that which generally hath been already answered may serve for answer to that exception which in these two respects they take

particularly against the form of our common prayer. To say that
in nothing they may be followed which are of the church of Rome
were violent and extreme. Some things they do in that they are
men, in that they are wise men and Christian men some things,
some things in that they are men misled and blinded with error.
As far as they follow reason and truth, we fear not to tread the
selfsame steps wherein they have gone, and to be their followers.
Where Rome keepeth that which is ancienter and better, others
whom we much more affect leaving it for newer and changing
it for worse; we had rather follow the perfections of them whom
we like not, than in defects resemble them whom we love.

(V.xxviii.1)

40   MINISTERIAL ATTIRE

XXIX. The attire which the minister of God is by order to use
at times of divine service being but a matter of mere formality,
yet such as for comeliness sake hath hitherto been judged by the
wiser sort of men not unnecessary to concur with other sensible
notes betokening the different kind or quality of persons and
actions whereto it is tied: as we think not ourselves the holier
because we use it, so neither should they with whom no such
thing is in use think us therefore unholy, because we submit
ourselves unto that, which in a matter so indifferent the wisdom
of authority and law have thought comely. To solemn actions of
royalty and justice their suitable ornaments are a beauty. Are
they only in religion a stain?   (V.xxix.1)

41   GESTURE AND POSITION IN WORSHIP

XXX. Having thus disputed whether the surplice be a fit garment to be used in the service of God, the next question whereinto
we are drawn is, whether it be a thing allowable or no that the

minister should say service in the chancel, or turn his face at any time from the people, or before service ended remove from the place where it was begun. By them which trouble us with these doubts we would more willingly be resolved of a greater doubt; whether it be not a kind of taking God's name in vain to debase religion with such frivolous disputes, a sin to bestow time and labour about them. Things of so mean regard and quality, although necessary to be ordered, are notwithstanding very unsavoury when they come to be disputed of: because disputation presupposeth some difficulty in the matter which is argued, whereas in things of this nature they must be either very simple or very froward who need to be taught by disputation what is meet. [V.xxx.1)

42 THE PSALMS

[2] The Prophet David having therefore singular knowledge not in poetry alone but in music also, judged them both to be things most necessary for the house of God, left behind him to that purpose a number of divinely indited poems, and was farther the author of adding unto poetry melody in public prayer, melody both vocal and instrumental, for the raising up of men's hearts, and the sweetening of their affections towards God. In which considerations the Church of Christ doth likewise at this present day retain it as an ornament to God's service, and an help to our own devotion. They which, under pretence of the Law ceremonial abrogated, require the abrogation of instrumental music, approving nevertheless the use of vocal melody to remain, must shew some reason wherefore the one should be thought a legal ceremony and not the other.

[3] In church music curiosity and ostentation of art, wanton or light or unsuitable harmony, such as only pleaseth the ear, and doth not naturally serve to the very kind and degree of those impressions, which the matter that goeth with it leaveth or is apt to leave in men's minds, doth rather blemish and disgrace that

we do than add either beauty or furtherance unto it. On the other side, these faults prevented, the force and efficacy of the thing itself, when it drowneth not utterly but fitly suiteth with matter altogether sounding to the praise of God, is in truth most admirable, and doth much edify if not the understanding because it teacheth not, yet surely the affection, because therein it worketh much. They must have hearts very dry and tough, from whom the melody of psalms doth not sometime draw that wherein a mind religiously affected delighteth.... (V.xxxviii.2, 3)

43 PETITIONARY PRAYERS

[2] Minds religiously affected are wont in every thing of weight and moment which they do or see, to examine according unto rules of piety what dependency it hath on God, what reference to themselves, what coherence with any of those duties whereunto all things in the world should lead, and accordingly they frame the inward disposition of their minds sometime to admire God, sometime to bless him and give him thanks, sometime to exult in his love, sometime to implore his mercy. All which different elevations of spirit unto God are contained in the name of prayer. Every good and holy desire though it lack the form, hath notwithstanding in itself the substance and with him the force of a prayer, who regardeth the very moanings, groans, and sighs of the heart of man. Petitionary prayer belongeth only to such as are in themselves impotent, and stand in need of relief from others. We thereby declare unto God what our own desire is that he by his power should effect. It presupposeth therefore in us first the want of that which we pray for; secondly, a feeling of that want; thirdly, an earnest willingness of mind to be eased therein; fourthly, a declaration of this our desire in the sight of God, not as if he should be otherwise ignorant of our necessities, but because we this way shew that we honour him as our God, and are verily persuaded that no good thing can come to pass which he by his omnipotent power effecteth not.

[3] Now because there is no man's prayer acceptable whose person is odious, neither any man's person gracious without faith, it is of necessity required that they which pray do believe. The prayers which our Lord and Saviour made were for his own worthiness accepted; ours God accepteth not but with this condition, if they be joined with belief in Christ.

The prayers of the just are accepted always, but not always those things granted for which they pray. For in prayer if faith and assurance to obtain were both one and the same thing, seeing that the effect of not obtaining is a plain testimony that they which prayed were not sure they should obtain, it would follow that their prayer being without certainty of the event, was also made unto God without faith, and consequently that God abhorred it. Which to think of so many prayers of saints as we find have failed in particular requests, how absurd were it! His faithful people have this comfort, that whatsoever they rightly ask, the same no doubt but they shall receive, so far as may stand with the glory of God, and their own everlasting good, unto either of which two it is no virtuous man's purpose to seek or desire to obtain any thing prejudicial, and therefore that clause which our Lord and Saviour in the prayer of his agony did express, we in petitions of like nature do always imply, *Pater, si possibile est*, "If it may stand with thy will and pleasure". Or if not, but that there be secret impediments and causes in regard whereof the thing we pray for is denied us, yet the prayer itself which we make is a pleasing sacrifice to God, who both accepteth and rewardeth it some other way. So that sinners in very truth are denied when they seem to prevail in their supplications [Numbers xi.33; 1 Samuel vii.7; Job i.12; Luke viii.32], because it is not for their sakes or to their good that their suits take place; the faithful contrariwise, because it is for their good oftentimes that their petitions do not take place, prevail even then when they most seem denied [2 Cor. xii.7-9]. "Our Lord God in anger hath granted some impatient men's requests, as on the other side the Apostle's suit he hath of favour and mercy not granted", saith St. Augustine.[1]

---

1   St. Augustine, *Epistle to the Widow Proba*, 121.

[4] To think we may pray unto God for nothing but what he hath promised in Holy Scripture we shall obtain, is perhaps an error. For of prayer there are two uses. It serveth as a mean to procure those things which God hath promised to grant when we ask; and it serveth as a mean to express our lawful desires also towards that, which whether we shall have or no we know not till we see the event. Things in themselves unholy or unseemly we may not ask; we may whatsoever being not forbidden either nature or grace shall reasonably move us to wish as importing the good of men, albeit God himself have nowhere by promise assured us of that particular which our prayer craveth. To pray for that which is in itself and of its own nature apparently a thing impossible, were not convenient. Wherefore though men do without offence wish daily that the affairs which with evil success are past might have fallen out much better, yet to pray that they may have been any other than they are, this being a manifest impossibility in itself, the rules of religion do not permit. Whereas contrariwise when things of their own nature contingent and mutable are by the secret determination of God appointed one way, though we the other way make our prayers, and consequently ask those things of God which are *by this supposition* impossible, we notwithstanding do not hereby in prayer transgress our lawful bounds. (V.xlviii.2-4)

44 THE SACRAMENTS

L. Instruction and Prayer whereof we have hitherto spoken, are duties which serve as elements, parts, or principles, to the rest that follow, in which number the Sacraments of the Church are chief. The Church is to us that very mother of our new birth [Gal. iv.26; Isaiah liv.3], in whose bowels we are all bred, at whose breasts we receive nourishment. As many therefore as are apparently to our judgment born of God, they have the seed of their regeneration by the ministry of the Church which useth to that end and purpose not only the Word, but the Sacraments, both having generative force and virtue.

[2] As oft as we mention a Sacrament properly understood, (for in the writings of the ancient Fathers all articles which are peculiar to Christian faith, all duties of religion containing that which sense or natural reason cannot of itself discern, are most commonly named Sacraments), our restraint of the word to some few principal divine ceremonies importeth in every such ceremony two things, the substance of the ceremony itself which is visible, and besides that somewhat else more secret in reference whereunto we conceive that ceremony to be a Sacrament. For we all admire and honour the holy Sacraments, not respecting so much the service which we do unto God in receiving them, as the dignity of that sacred and secret gift which we thereby receive from God. Seeing that Sacraments therefore consist altogether in relation to some such gift or grace supernatural as only God can bestow, how should any but the Church administer those ceremonies as Sacraments which are not thought to be Sacraments by any but by the Church?

[3] There is in Sacraments to be observed their force and their form of administration. Upon their force their necessity dependeth. So that how they are necessary we cannot discern till we see how effectual they are. When Sacraments are said to be visible signs of invisible grace, we thereby conceive how grace is indeed the very end for which these heavenly mysteries were instituted, and besides sundry other properties observed in them, the matter whereof they consist is such as signifieth, figureth, and representeth their end. But still their efficacy resteth obscure to our understanding, except we search somewhat more distinctly what grace in particular that is whereunto they are referred, and what manner of operation they have towards it.

The use of Sacraments is but only in this life, yet so that here they concern a far better life than this, and are for that cause accompanied with "grace which worketh Salvation". Sacraments are the powerful instruments of God to eternal life. For as our natural life consisteth in the union of the body with the soul; so our life supernatural in the union of the soul with God. And forasmuch as there is no union of God with man without that mean between both which is both, it seemeth requisite that we first consider how God is in Christ, then how Christ is in us, and how the Sacraments do serve to make us partakers of Christ. In other things we may be more brief, but the weight of these requireth largeness.   (V.l)

45 THE IMPORTANCE OF THE INCARNATION

LI. "The Lord our God is but one God". In which indivisible unity notwithstanding we adore the Father as being altogether of himself, we glorify that consubstantial Word which is the Son, we bless and magnify that co-essential Spirit eternally proceeding from both which is the Holy Ghost. Seeing therefore the Father is of none, the Son is of the Father and the Spirit is of both, they are by these their several properties really distinguishable each from other. For the substance of God with this property *to be of none* doth make the Person of the Father; the very selfsame substance in number with this property *to be of the Father* maketh the Person of the Son; the same substance having added unto it the property of *proceeding from the other two* maketh the Person of the Holy Ghost. So that in every Person there is implied both the substance of God which is one, and also that property which causeth the same person really and truly to differ from the other two. Every person hath his own subsistence which no other besides hath, although there be others besides that are of the same substance. As no man but Peter can be the person which Peter is, yet Paul hath the selfsame nature which Peter hath. Again, angels have every of them the nature of pure and invisible spirits, but every angel is not that angel which appeared in a dream to Joseph.

[2] Now when God became man, lest we should err in applying this to the Person of the Father, or of the Spirit, St. Peter's confession unto Christ was, "Thou art *the Son* of the living God" [Matthew xvi.16], and St. John's exposition thereof was plain, that it is *the Word* which was made Flesh [John i.14]. "The Father and the

Holy Ghost (saith Damascen) have no communion with the incarnation of the Word otherwise than only by approbation and assent".[1]

Notwithstanding, forasmuch as the Word and Deity are one subject, we must beware we exclude not the nature of God from incarnation, and so make the Son of God incarnate not to be very God. For undoubtedly even the nature of God itself in the only person of the Son is incarnate, and hath taken to itself flesh. Wherefore incarnation may neither be granted to any person but only one, nor yet denied to that nature which is common unto all three.

[3] Concerning the cause of which incomprehensible mystery, forasmuch as it seemeth a thing unconsonant that the world should honour any other as the Saviour but him whom it honoureth as the Creator of the world, and in the wisdom of God it hath not been thought convenient to admit any way of saving man but by man himself, though nothing should be spoken of the love and mercy of God towards man, which this way are become such a spectacle as neither men nor angels can behold without a kind of heavenly astonishment, we may hereby perceive there is cause sufficient why divine nature should assume human, that so God might be in Christ reconciling to himself the world [2 Cor. v.19]. And if some cause be likewise required why rather to this end and purpose the Son than either the Father or the Holy Ghost should be made man, could we which are born the children of wrath be adopted the sons of God through grace, any other than the natural Son of God being Mediator between God and us? It became therefore him by whom all things are to be the way of salvation to all, that the institution and restitution of the world might be both wrought by one hand [Hebrews ii.10]. The world's salvation was without the incarnation of the Son of God a thing impossible, not simply impossible, but impossible it being presupposed that the will of God was no otherwise to have it saved than by the death of his own Son. Wherefore taking to himself our flesh, and by his incarnation making it his own

1   Damascen, *De Orthodoxia Fide*, III.11.

flesh, he had now of his own although from us what to offer unto God for us.

And as Christ took manhood that by it he might be capable of death whereunto he humbled himself, so because manhood is the proper subject of compassion and feeling pity, which maketh the sceptre of Christ's regency even in the kingdom of heaven amiable, he which without our nature could not on earth suffer for the sins of the world, doth now also by means thereof both make intercession to God for sinners and exercise dominion over all men with a true, a natural, and a sensible touch of mercy [Hebrews iv.15].   (V.li)

46   THE COMMUNION OF SAINTS

[7] They which thus were in God eternally by their intended admission to life, have by vocation or adoption God actually now in them, as the artificer is in the work which his hand doth presently frame. Life as all other gifts and benefits groweth originally from the Father, and cometh not to us but by the Son [1 John v.11], nor by the Son to any of us in particular but through the Spirit [Romans viii.10]. For this cause the Apostle wisheth to the church of Corinth, "The grace of our Lord Jesus Christ, and the love of God, and the fellowship of the Holy Ghost" [2 Cor. xiii.13]. Which three St. Peter comprehendeth in one, "The participation of divine Nature" [2 Peter i.4]. We are therefore in God through Christ eternally according to that intent and purpose whereby we were chosen to be made his in this present world before the world itself was made, we are in God through the knowledge which is had of us, and the love which is borne towards us from everlasting. But in God we actually are no longer than only from the time of our actual adoption into the body of his true Church, into the fellowship of his children. For his Church he knoweth and loveth, so that they which are in the Church are thereby known to be in him. Our being in Christ by eternal foreknowledge saveth us not without our actual and real adoption into the fellow-

ship of his saints in this present world. For in him we actually are by our actual incorporation into that society which hath him for their Head [Col. ii.10], and doth make together with him one Body, (he and they in that respect having one name) [1 Cor. xii.12], for which cause, by virtue of this mystical conjunction, we are of him and in him even as though our very flesh and bones should be made continuate with his [Eph. v.30]. We are in Christ because he knoweth and loveth us even as parts of himself [John xv.9]. No man actually is in him but they in whom he actually is. For "he which hath not the Son of God hath not life" [1 John v.12]. "I am the vine and you are the branches: he which abideth in me and I in him the same bringeth forth much fruit"; but the branch severed from the vine withereth. [John xv.5-6]. We are therefore adopted sons of God to eternal life by participation of the only-begotten Son of God, whose life is the well-spring and cause of ours [John xiv.15; Eph. v.23].

It is too cold an interpretation, whereby some men expound our being in Christ to import nothing else, but only that the selfsame nature which maketh us to be men, is in him, and maketh him man as we are. For what man in the world is there which hath not so far forth communion with Jesus Christ? It is not this that can sustain the weight of such sentences as speak of the mystery of our coherence with Jesus Christ [John xiv.20; xv.4]. The Church is in Christ as Eve was in Adam. Yea by grace we are every of us in Christ and in his Church, as by nature we are in those our first parents. God made Eve of the rib of Adam. And his Church he frameth out of the very flesh, the very wounded and bleeding side of the Son of man. His body crucified and his blood shed for the life of the world, are the true elements of that heavenly being, which maketh us such as himself is of whom we come [1 Cor. xv.48]. For which cause the words of Adam may be fitly the words of Christ concerning his Church, "flesh of my flesh, and bone of my bones", a true native extract out of mine own body. So that in him even according to his manhood we according to our heavenly being are as branches in that root out of which they grow.

To all things he is life, and to men light [John i.4-9], *as the Son of God;* to the Church both life and light eternal [John vi.57] by being made the Son of Man for us, and by being in us a Saviour, whether we respect him as God, or as man. Adam is in us as an original cause of our nature, and of that corruption of nature which causeth death, Christ as the cause original of restoration to life [Hebrews v.9]; the person of Adam is not in us, but his nature, and the corruption of his nature derived into all men by propagation; Christ having Adam's nature as we have, but incorrupt, deriveth not nature but incorruption and that immediately from his own person into all that belong unto him. As therefore we are really partakers of the body of sin and death received from Adam, so except we be truly partakers of Christ, and as really possessed of his Spirit, all we speak of eternal life is but a dream.

[8] That which quickeneth us is the Spirit of the second Adam [1 Cor. xv, 22, 45], and his flesh that wherewith he quickeneth. That which in him made our nature uncorrupt, was the union of his Deity with our nature. And in that respect the sentence of death and condemnation which only taketh hold upon sinful flesh, could no way possibly extend unto him. This caused his voluntary death for others to prevail with God, and to have the force of an expiatory sacrifice. The blood of Christ, as the Apostle witnesseth, doth therefore take away sin, because "through the eternal Spirit he offered himself unto God without spot" [Hebrews v.14]. That which sanctified our nature in Christ, that which made it a sacrifice available to take away sin, is the same which quickeneth it, raised it out of the grave after death, and exalted it unto glory. Seeing therefore that Christ is in us as a quickening Spirit, the first degree of communion with Christ must needs consist in the participation of his Spirit, which Cyprian in that respect well termeth *germanissimam societatem,*[1] the highest and truest society that can be between man and him which is both God and man in one.   (V.lvi.7-8)

1 Cyprian, *De Coena Domini,* c.6

47   THE NECESSITY OF THE SACRAMENTS

LVII. It greatly offendeth, that some, when they labour to shew the use of the holy Sacraments, assign unto them no end but only *to teach* the mind, by other senses, that which the Word doth teach by hearing. Whereupon, how easily neglect and careless regard of so heavenly mysteries may follow, we see in part by some experience had of those men with whom that opinion is most strong. For where the word of God may be heard, which teacheth with much more expedition and more full explication any thing we have to learn, if all the benefit we reap by sacraments be instruction, they which at all times have opportunity of using the better mean to that purpose, will surely hold the worse in less estimation. And unto infants which are not capable of instruction, who would not think it a mere superfluity that any sacrament is administered, if to administer the sacraments be but to teach receivers what God doth for them? There is of sacraments therefore undoubtedly some other more excellent and heavenly use.

[2] Sacraments, by reason of their mixed nature, are more diversely interpreted and disputed of than any other part of religion besides, for that in so great store of properties belonging to the selfsame thing, as every man's wit hath taken hold of some especial consideration above the rest, so they have accordingly seemed one to cross another as touching their several opinions about the necessity of sacraments, whereas in truth their disagreement is not great. For let respect be had to the duty which every communicant doth undertake, and we may well determine concerning the use of sacraments, that they serve as bonds of obedience to God, strict obligations to the mutual exercise of Christian charity, provocations to godliness, preservations from sin, memorials of the principal benefits of Christ; respect the time of their institution, and it thereby appeareth that God hath annexed them for ever unto the New Testament, as other rites were before with the Old; regard the weakness which is in us, and they are warrants for the more security of our belief; compare the receivers of them with such as receive them not, and sacraments

are marks of distinction to separate God's own from strangers: so that in all these respects, they are found to be most necessary.

[3] But their chiefest force and virtue consisteth not herein so much as in that they are heavenly ceremonies, which God hath sanctified and ordained to be administered in his Church, first, as marks whereby to know when God doth impart the vital or saving grace of Christ unto all that are capable thereof, and secondly as means conditional which God requireth in them unto whom he imparteth grace. For sith God in himself is invisible, and cannot by us be discerned working, therefore when it seemeth good in the eyes of his heavenly wisdom, that men for some special intent and purpose should take notice of his glorious presence, he giveth them some plain and sensible token whereby to know what they cannot see. For Moses to see God and live was impossible, yet Moses by fire knew where the glory of God extraordinarily was present [Exodus iii.2]. The angel, by whom God endued the waters of the pool called Bethesda with supernatural virtue to heal, was not seen of any, yet the time of the angel's presence known by the troubled motions of the waters themselves [John v.4]. The Apostles by fiery tongues which they saw, were admonished when the Spirit, which they could not behold, was upon them [Acts ii.3]. In like manner it is with us. Christ and his Holy Spirit with all their blessed effects, though entering into the soul of man we are not able to apprehend or express how, do notwithstanding give notice of the times when they use to make their access, because it pleaseth Almighty God to communicate by sensible means those blessings which are incomprehensible.

[4] Seeing therefore that grace is a consequent of sacraments, a thing which accompanieth them as their end, a benefit which he that hath receiveth from God himself the author of sacraments, and not from any other natural or supernatural quality in them, it may be hereby both understood that sacraments are necessary, and that the manner of their necessity to life supernatural is not in all respects as food unto natural life, because they contain *in themselves* no vital force or efficacy, they are not physical but *moral instruments* of salvation, duties of service and worship, which

unless we perform as the Author of grace requireth, they are unprofitable. For all receive not the grace of God which receive the sacraments of his grace.[1] Neither is it *ordinarily* his will to bestow the grace of sacraments on any, but by the sacraments; which grace also they that receive by sacraments or with sacraments, receive it from him and not from them. For of sacraments the very same is true which Salomon's wisdom observeth in the brazen serpent, "He that turned towards it was not healed by the thing he saw, but by thee, O Saviour of all" [Wisdom xvi.7].

[5] This is therefore the necessity of sacraments. That saving grace which Christ originally is or hath for the general good of his whole Church, by sacraments he severally deriveth into every member thereof. Sacraments serve as the instruments of God to that end and purpose, moral instruments, the use whereof is in our hands, the effect in his; for the use we have his express commandment, for the effect his conditional promise: so that without our obedience to the one, there is of the other no apparent assurance, as contrariwise where the signs and sacraments of his grace are not either through contempt unreceived, or received with contempt, we are not to doubt but that they really give what they promise, and are what they signify. For we take not baptism nor the eucharist for bare *resemblances* or memorials of things absent, neither for *naked signs* and testimonies assuring us of grace received before, but (as they are indeed and in verity) for means effectual whereby God when we take the sacraments delivereth into our hands that grace available unto eternal life, which grace the sacraments represent or signify.

[6] There have grown in the doctrine concerning sacraments many difficulties for want of distinct explication what kind or degree of grace doth belong unto each sacrament. For by this it hath come to pass, that the true immediate cause why Baptism, and why the Supper of our Lord is necessary, few do rightly and distinctly consider. It cannot be denied but sundry the same effects and benefits which grow unto men by the one sacrament may rightly be attributed unto the other. Yet then doth baptism

1 St. Augustine, *On Psalms*, 70 (77).

challenge to itself but the inchoation of those graces, the consummation whereof dependeth on mysteries ensuing. We receive Christ Jesus in baptism once as the first beginner, in the eucharist often as being by continual degrees the finisher of our life. By baptism therefore we receive Christ Jesus, and from him that saving grace which is proper unto baptism. By the other sacrament we receive him also, imparting therein himself and that grace which the eucharist properly bestoweth. So that each sacrament having both that which is general or common, and that also which is peculiar unto itself, we may hereby gather that the participation of Christ which properly belongeth to any one sacrament, is not otherwise to be obtained but by the sacrament whereunto it is proper.   (V.lvii)

48   THE THREE ESSENTIALS OF A SACRAMENT

[2] In writing and speaking of the blessed sacraments we use for the most part under the name of their *substance* not only to comprise that whereof they outwardly and sensibly consist, but also the secret grace which they signify and exhibit. This is the reason wherefore commonly in definitions, whether they be framed larger to augment, or stricter to abridge the number of sacraments, we find grace expressly mentioned as their true essential form, elements as the matter whereunto that form doth adjoin itself. But if that be separated which is secret, and that considered alone which is seen, as of necessity it must in all those speeches that make distinction of sacraments from sacramental grace, the name of sacrament in such speeches can imply no more than what the *outward substance* thereof doth comprehend. And to make complete the outward substance of a sacrament, there is required an outward form, which form sacramental elements receive from sacramental words. Hereupon it groweth, that many times there are three things said to make up the substance of a sacrament, namely, the grace which is thereby offered, the element which shadoweth or signifieth grace, and the word which

expresseth what is done by the element. So that whether we consider the outward by itself alone, or both the outward and inward substance of any sacrament; there are in the one respect but two essential parts, and in the other but three that concur to give sacraments their full being.   (V.lviii.2)

49   BAPTISM

[1] The true necessity of baptism a few propositions considered will soon decide. All things which either are known *causes* or set *means*, whereby any great good is usually procured, or men delivered from grievous evil, the same we must needs confess necessary. And, if regeneration were not in this very sense a thing necessary to eternal life, would Christ himself have taught Nicodemus that to see the kingdom of God is impossible, saving only for those men which are born from above? [John iii.3].

His words following in the next sentence are a proof sufficient, that to our regeneration his Spirit is no less necessary than regeneration itself necessary unto life [John iii.5].

Thirdly, unless as the Spirit is a necessary inward cause, so Water were a necessary outward mean to our regeneration, what construction should we give unto those words wherein we are said to be new-born, and that ἐξ ὕδατος, even of *water*? Why are we taught that with water God doth purify and cleanse his Church? [Eph. v.26]. Wherefore do the Apostles of Christ term baptism a bath of regeneration? [Titus iii.5]. What purpose had they in giving men advice to receive outward baptism, and in persuading them it did avail to remission of sins? [Acts ii.38].

[2] If outward baptism were a cause in itself possessed of that power either natural or supernatural, without the present operation whereof no such effect could possibly grow, it must then follow, that seeing effects do never prevent the necessary causes out of which they spring, no man could ever receive grace before baptism: which being apparently both known and also confessed to be otherwise in many particulars, although in the rest we make

not baptism a cause of grace, yet the grace which is given them with their baptism doth so far forth depend on the very outward sacrament, that God will have it embraced not only as a sign or token what we receive, but also as an instrument or mean whereby we receive grace, because baptism is a sacrament which God hath instituted in his Church, to the end that they which receive the same might thereby be incorporated into Christ, and so through his most precious merit obtain as well that saving grace of imputation which taketh away all former guiltiness, as also that infused divine virtue of the Holy Ghost, which giveth to the powers of the soul their first disposition towards future newness of life.

[3] There are that elevate too much the ordinary and immediate means of life, relying wholly upon the bare conceit of that eternal election, which notwithstanding includeth a subordination of means without which we are not actually brought to enjoy what God secretly did intend; and therefore to build upon God's election if we keep not ourselves to the ways which he hath appointed for men to walk in, is but a self-deceiving vanity. When the Apostle saw men called to the participation of Jesus Christ, after the Gospel of God embraced and the sacrament of life received, he feareth not then to put them in the number of elect saints [Eph. i.1), he then accounteth them delivered from death, and clean purged from all sin [Eph. v.8]. Till then notwithstanding their pre-ordination unto life which none could know of saving God, what were they in the Apostle's own account but children of wrath as well as others, plain aliens altogether without hope, strangers utterly without God in this present world? [Eph. ii.3, 12]. So that by sacraments and other sensible tokens of grace we may boldly gather that he, whose mercy vouchsafeth now to bestow the means, hath also long sithence intended us that whereunto they lead. But let us never think it safe to presume of our own last end by bare conjectural collections of his first intent and purpose, the means failing that should come between. Predestination bringeth not to life, without the grace of external vocation, wherein our baptism is implied [Romans viii.30]. For as we are not naturally men without birth, so neither are we

Christian men in the eyes of the Church of God but by new birth, nor according to the manifest ordinary course of divine dispensation new-born, but by that baptism which both declareth and maketh us Christians. In which respect we justly hold it to be the door of our actual entrance into God's house, the first apparent beginning of life,[1] a seal perhaps to the grace of Election, before received, but to our sanctification here a step that hath not any before it.... Baptism is an action in part moral, in part ecclesiastical, and in part mystical: moral, as being a duty which men perform towards God; ecclesiastical, in that it belongeth unto God's Church as a public duty; finally mystical, if we respect what God doth thereby intend to work.

The greatest moral perfection of baptism consisteth in men's devout obedience to the law of God, which law requireth both the outward act or thing done, and also that religious affection which God doth so much regard, that without it whatsoever we do is hateful in his sight, who therefore is said to respect *adverbs* more than *verbs*, because the end of his law in appointing what we shall do is our own perfection, which perfection consisteth chiefly in the virtuous disposition of the mind, and approveth itself to him not by *doing* but by doing *well*. Wherein appeareth also the difference between human and divine laws, the one of which two are content with *opus operatum*, the other require *opus operantis*, the one do but claim the deed, the other especially the mind. So that according to laws which principally respect the heart of men, works of religion being not religiously performed, cannot morally be perfect.

Baptism as an ecclesiastical work is for the manner of performance ordered by divers ecclesiastical laws, providing that as the sacrament itself is a gift of no mean worth, so the ministry thereof might in all circumstances appear to be a function of no small regard.

All that belongeth to the mystical perfection of baptism outwardly, is the element, the word, and the serious application of both unto him which receiveth both; whereunto if we add that

1   Basil, *De Spiritu Sancto*, c.10.

secret reference which this action hath to life and remission of
sins by virtue of Christ's own compact solemnly made with his
Church, to accomplish fully the Sacrament of Baptism, there is
not any thing more required.

Now put the question whether baptism administered to infants
without any spiritual calling be unto them both a true sacrament
and an effectual instrument of grace, or else an act of no more
account than the ordinary washings are? The sum of all that can
be said to defeat such baptism is, that those things which have
no being can work nothing, and that baptism without the power
of ordination is as judgment without sufficient jurisdiction, void,
frustrate, and of no effect.[1] But to this we answer, that the fruit
of baptism dependeth only upon the covenant which God hath
made; that God by covenant requireth in the elder sort Faith and
Baptism, in children the Sacrament of Baptism alone, whereunto
he hath also given them right by special privilege of birth within
the bosom of the holy Church; that infants therefore, which have
received baptism complete as touching the mystical perfection
thereof, are by virtue of his own covenant and promise cleansed
from all sin, forasmuch as all other laws concerning that which
in baptism is either moral or ecclesiastical do bind the Church
which giveth baptism, and not the infant which receiveth it of
the Church. So that if any thing be therein amiss, the harm which
groweth by violation of holy ordinances must altogether rest where
the bonds of such ordinances hold.   (V.lx.1-3; lxii.15)

50   INADMISSIBILITY OF FEMALE MINISTRY

[2] To make women teachers in the house of God were a gross
absurdity, seeing the Apostle hath said, "I permit not a woman
to teach" [1 Tim. ii.2]; and again, "Let your women in churches
be silent" [1 Cor, xiv.34]. Those extraordinary gifts of speaking
with tongues and prophesying, which God at that time did not

1   Cartwright, III.128.

only bestow upon men, but on women also, made it the harder to hold them confined with private bounds. Whereupon the Apostle's ordinance was necessary against women's public admission to teach. And because when law hath begun some one thing or other well, it giveth good occasion either to draw by judicious exposition out of the very law itself, or to annex to the law by authority and jurisdiction things of like conveniency, therefore Clement extendeth this apostolic constitution to baptism. "For," saith he, "if we have denied them leave to teach, how should any man dispense with nature and make them ministers of holy things, seeing this unskilfulness is a part of the Grecians' impiety, which for the service of women goddesses have women priests?"[1]   (V.lxii.2)

51   ACCEPTANCE FOR BAPTISM NOT DEPENDENT ON CHRISTIAN PARENTAGE

[5] ... A wrong conceit, that none may receive the sacrament of baptism but they whose parents, at the least one of them, are by the soundness of their religion and by their virtuous demeanour known to be men of God, hath caused some to repel children, whosoever bring them, if their parents be mispersuaded in religion, or for other misdeserts excommunicated;[2] some likewise for that cause to withhold baptism, unless the father, albeit no such exception can justly be taken against him, do notwithstanding make profession of his faith, and avouch the child to be his own. Thus whereas God hath appointed them ministers of holy things, they make themselves inquisitors of men's persons a great deal farther than need is.

They should consider that God hath ordained baptism in favour of mankind. To restrain favours is an odious thing, to enlarge them acceptable both to God and man. Whereas therefore

1   Clement, *Apostolic Constitutions*, III, 9.
2   Cartwright, I, 172.

the civil law gave divers immunities to them which were fathers of three children and had them living, those immunities they held although their children were all dead, if war had consumed them, because it seemed in that case not against reason to repute them by a courteous construction of law as live men, in that the honour of their service done to the commonwealth would remain always. Can it hurt us in exhibiting the graces which God doth bestow on men, or can it prejudice his glory, if the selfsame equity guide and direct our hands?

When God made his covenant with such as had Abraham to their father, was only Abraham's immediate issue, or only his lineal posterity according to the flesh included in that covenant? Were not proselytes as well as Jews always taken for the sons of Abraham? Yea because the very heads of families are fathers in some sort as touching providence and care for the meanest that belong unto them, the servants which Abraham had bought with money were as capable of circumcision, being newly born, as any natural child that Abraham himself begat.

Be it then that baptism belongeth to none but such as either believe presently, or else being infants are the children of *believing parents*. In case the Church do bring children to the holy font whose natural parents are either unknown, or known to be such as the church accurseth, but yet forgetteth not in that severity to take compassion upon their offspring, (for it is the Church which doth offer them to baptism by the ministry of presentors), were it not against both equity and duty to refuse the mother of believers herself, and not to take her in this case for a faithful parent? It is not the virtue of our fathers nor the faith of any other that can give us the true holiness which we have by virtue of our new birth. Yet even through the common faith and spirit of God's Church, (a thing which no quality of parents can prejudice), I say through the faith of the Church of God undertaking the motherly care of our souls, so far forth we may be and are in our infancy sanctified, as to be thereby made sufficiently capable of baptism, and to be interested in the rites of our new birth for their piety's sake that offer us thereunto.   (V.lxiv.5)

52   THE SIGN OF THE CROSS IN BAPTISM
AND THE VALUE OF SIGNS AND CEREMONIES

LXV. In baptism many things of very ancient continuance are now quite and clean abolished, for that the virtue and grace of this sacrament had been therewith overshadowed, as fruit with too great abundance of leaves. Notwithstanding to them which think it always imperfect reformation that doth but shear and not flay, our retaining certain of those former rites, especially the *dangerous* sign of the cross, hath seemed almost an impardonable oversight. "The cross," they say, "sith it is but a mere invention of man, should not therefore at all have been added to the sacrament of baptism. To sign children's foreheads with a cross, in token that hereafter they shall not be ashamed to make profession of the faith of Christ, is to bring into the Church a new word, whereas there ought to be no Doctor heard in the Church but our Saviour Christ. That reason which moved the Fathers to use, should move us not to use, the sign of the cross. They lived with heathens which had the cross of Christ in contempt, we with such as adore the cross, and therefore we ought to abandon it even as in like consideration Ezechias did of old the brazen serpent".[1]

[2] These are the causes of displeasure conceived against the cross, a ceremony the use whereof hath been profitable although we observe it not as the ordinance of God but of man. For, saith Tertullian, "if of this and the like customs thou shouldest require some commandment to be shewed thee out of Scriptures, there is none found".[2] What reason there is to justify tradition, use or custom in this behalf, "either thou mayest of thyself perceive, or else learn of some other that doth". Lest therefore the name of tradition should be offensive to any, considering how far by some it hath been and is abused, we mean by traditions, ordinances made in the prime of Christian religion, established with that authority which Christ hath left to his Church for matters indifferent, and in that consideration requisite to be observed, till like

1   Cartwright, I, 135-6 (abridged), 170-71.
2   Tertullian, *De Corona Militis*, c.4.

authority see just and reasonable cause to alter them. So that traditions ecclesiastical are not rudely and in gross to be shaken off, because the inventors of them were men.

[4] Ceremonies have more in weight than in sight, they work by commonness of use much, although in the several acts of their usage we scarcely discern any good they do. And because the use which they have for the most part is not perfectly understood, superstition is apt to impute unto them greater virtue than indeed they have. For prevention whereof when we use this ceremony we always plainly express the end whereunto it serveth, namely, for a sign of remembrance to put us in mind of our duty.

(V.lxv.1-2, 4)

53   THE EUCHARIST

LXVII. The grace which we have by the holy Eucharist doth not begin but continue life. No man therefore receiveth this sacrament before Baptism, because no dead thing is capable of nourishment. That which groweth must of necessity first live. If our bodies did not daily waste, food to restore them were a thing superfluous. And it may be that the grace of baptism would serve to eternal life, were it not that the state of our spiritual being is daily so much hindered and impaired after baptism. In that life therefore where neither body nor soul can decay, our souls shall as little require this sacrament as our bodies corporal nourishment. But as long as the days of our warfare last, during the time that we are both subject to diminution and capable of augmentation in grace, the words of our Lord and Saviour Christ will remain forcible, "Except ye eat the flesh of the Son of man, and drink his blood, ye have no life in you" [John vi.33].

Life being therefore proposed unto all men as their end, they which by baptism have laid the foundation and attained the first beginning of a new life have here their nourishment and food prescribed for *continuance of life* in them. Such as will live the life of God must eat the flesh and drink the blood of the Son of man, because this is a part of that diet which if we want we cannot live. Whereas therefore in our infancy we are incorporated into Christ and by Baptism receive the grace of his Spirit without any sense or feeling of the gift which God bestoweth, in the Eucharist we so receive the gift of God, that we know by grace what the grace is which God giveth us, the degrees of our own increase in holiness and virtue we see and can judge of them, we understand that the strength of our life begun in Christ is Christ, that his flesh is meat and his blood drink, not by surmised imagination but truly, even so truly that through faith we perceive in the body and blood sacramentally presented the very taste of eternal life, the grace of the sacrament is here as the food which we eat and drink.

[2] This was it that some did exceedingly fear, lest Zwinglius and Œcolampadius would bring to pass, that men should account of this sacrament but only as of a shadow, destitute, empty and void of Christ. But seeing that by opening the several opinions which have been held, they are grown for aught I can see on all sides at the length to a general agreement concerning that which alone is material, namely the *real participation* of Christ and of life in his body and blood *by means of this sacrament*; wherefore should the world continue still distracted and rent with so manifold contentions, when there remaineth now no controversy saving only about the subject *where* Christ is? Yea even in this point no side denieth but that *the soul of man* is the receptacle of Christ's presence. Whereby the question is yet driven to a narrower issue, nor doth any thing rest doubtful but this, whether when the sacrament is administered Christ be whole *within man only*, or else his body and blood be also externally seated in the very consecrated elements themselves; which opinion they that defend are driven either to *consubstantiate* and incorporate Christ with elements sacramental, or to *transubstantiate* and change their substance into his; and so the one to hold him really but invisibly moulded up with the substance of those elements, the other to hide him under the only visible show of bread and wine, the substance whereof as they imagine is abolished and his succeeded in the same room.

[3] All things considered and compared with that success which truth hath hitherto had by so bitter conflicts with errors in this point, shall I wish that men would more give themselves to meditate with silence what we have by the sacrament, and less to dispute of the manner how? If any man suppose that this were too great stupidity and dulness, let us see whether the Apostles of our Lord themselves have not done the like. It appeareth by many examples that they of their own disposition were very scrupulous and inquisitive, yea in other cases of less importance and less difficulty always apt to move questions. How cometh it to pass that so few words of so high a mystery being uttered, they receive with gladness the gift of Christ and make no show of doubt or scruple? The reason hereof is not dark to them which have any thing at all observed how the powers of the mind are wont to stir when that which we infinitely long for presenteth itself above and besides expectation. Curious and intricate speculations do hinder, they abate, they quench such inflamed motions of delight and joy as divine graces use to raise when extraordinarily they are present. The mind therefore feeling present joy is always marvellous unwilling to admit any other cogitation, and in that case casteth off those disputes whereunto the intellectual part at other times easily draweth.

A manifest effect whereof may be noted if we compare with our Lord's disciples in the twentieth of John the people that are said in the sixth of John to have gone after him to Capernaum. These leaving him on the one side of the sea of Tiberias, and finding him again as soon as themselves by ship were arrived on the contrary side, whither they knew that by ship he came not, and by land the journey was longer than according to the time he could have to travel, as they wondered so they asked also, "Rabbi, when camest thou hither?" [John vi.25]. The disciples when Christ appeared to them in far more strange and miraculous manner moved no question, but rejoiced greatly in that they saw. For why? The one sort beheld only that in Christ which they knew was more than natural, but yet their affection was not rapt therewith through any great extraordinary gladness, the other when they looked on Christ were not ignorant that they saw the wellspring of their own everlasting felicity; the one because they enjoyed not disputed, the other disputed not because they enjoyed.

[4] If then the presence of Christ with them did so much move, judge what their thoughts and affections were at the time of this new presentation of Christ not before their eyes but within their souls. They had learned before that his flesh and blood are the true cause of eternal life; that this they are not by the bare force of their own substance, but through the dignity and worth of his Person which offered them up by way of sacrifice for the life of the whole world, and doth make them still effectual thereunto; finally that to us they are life in particular, by being particularly received. Thus much they knew, although as yet they understood not perfectly to what effect or issue the same would come, till at the length being assembled for no other cause which they could imagine but to have eaten the Passover only that Moyses appointeth, when they saw their Lord and Master with hands and eyes lifted up to heaven first bless and consecrate for the endless good of all generations till the world's end the chosen elements of bread and wine, which elements made for ever the instruments of life by virtue of his divine benediction they being the first that were commanded to receive from him, the first which were warranted by his promise that not only unto them at the present time but to whomsoever they and their successors after them did duly administer the same, those mysteries should serve as conducts of life and conveyances of his body and blood unto them, was it possible they should hear that voice, "Take, eat, this is my body; drink ye all of this, this is my blood"; possible that doing what was required and believing what was promised, the same should have present effect in them, and not fill them with a kind of fearful admiration at the heaven which they saw in themselves? They had at that time a sea of comfort and joy to wade in, and we by that which they did are taught that this heavenly food is given for the satisfying of our empty souls, and not for the exercising of our curious and subtle wits.

[5] If we doubt what those admirable words may import, let him be our teacher for the meaning of Christ to whom Christ was

himself a schoolmaster, let our Lord's Apostle be his interpreter, content we ourselves with his explication, My body, *the communion of my body*, My blood, *the communion of my blood*. Is there any thing more expedite, clear, and easy, than that as Christ is termed our life because through him we obtain life, so the parts of this sacrament are his body and blood for that they are so to us who receiving them receive that by them which they are termed? The bread and cup are his body and blood because they are causes instrumental upon the receipt whereof the *participation* of his body and blood ensueth. For that which produceth any certain effect is not vainly nor improperly said to be that very effect whereunto it tendeth. Every cause is in the effect which groweth from it. Our souls and bodies quickened to eternal life are effects the cause whereof is the Person of Christ, his body and his blood are the true wellspring out of which this life floweth. So that his body and blood are in that very subject whereunto they minister life not only by effect or operation, even as the influence of the heavens is in plants, beasts, men, and in every thing which they quicken, but also by a far more divine and mystical kind of union, which maketh us one with him even as he and the Father are one.

[6] The real presence of Christ's most blessed body and blood is not therefore to be sought for in the sacrament, but in the worthy receiver of the sacrament.

And with this the very order of our Saviour's words agreeth, first "take and eat"; then "this is my Body which was broken for you": first "drink ye all of this"; then followeth "this is my Blood of the New Testament which is shed for many for the remission of sins" [Mark xiv.22]. I see not which way it should be gathered by the words of Christ, when and where the bread is His body or the cup His blood, but only in the very heart and soul of him which receiveth them. As for the sacraments, they really exhibit, but for aught we can gather out of that which is written of them, they are not really nor do really contain in themselves that grace which with them or by them it pleaseth God to bestow.

If on all sides it be confessed that the grace of Baptism is poured into the soul of man, that by water we receive it although it be neither seated in the water nor the water changed into it, what should induce men to think that the grace of the Eucharist must needs be in the Eucharist before it can be in us that receive it?

The fruit of the Eucharist is the participation of the body and blood of Christ. There is no sentence of Holy Scripture which saith that we cannot by this sacrament be made partakers of his body and blood except they be first contained in the sacrament, or the sacrament converted into them. "This is my body", and "this is my blood", being words of promise, sith we all agree that by the sacrament Christ doth really and truly in us perform his promise, why do we vainly trouble ourselves with so fierce contentions whether by consubstantiation, or else by transubstantiation the sacrament itself be first possessed with Christ, or no? A thing which no way can either further or hinder us howsoever it stand, because our participation of Christ in this sacrament dependeth on the co-operation of his omnipotent power which maketh it his body and blood to us, whether with change or without alteration of the element such as they imagine we need not greatly to care nor inquire.

[7] Take therefore that wherein all agree, and then consider by itself what cause why the rest in question should not rather be left as superfluous than urged as necessary. It is on all sides plainly confessed, first that this sacrament is a true and a real participation of Christ, who thereby imparteth himself even his whole entire Person *as a mystical Head* unto every soul that receiveth him, and that every such receiver doth thereby incorporate or unite himself unto Christ as *a mystical member of* him, yea of them also whom he acknowledgeth to be his own; secondly that to whom *the person of Christ* is thus communicated, to them he giveth by the same sacrament his Holy Spirit to sanctify them as it sanctifieth him which is their head; thirdly that what *merit, force or virtue soever there is in his sacrificed body and blood*, we freely, fully and wholly have it by this sacrament; fourthly that *the effect thereof in us is a real transmutation of our souls and bodies* from sin to righteousness, from death and corruption to immortality and life; fifthly that because the sacrament being of itself but a corruptible and earthly creature must needs be thought an unlikely instrument to work so admirable effects in man, we are therefore

to rest ourselves altogether upon *the strength of his glorious power* who is able and will bring to pass that the bread and cup which he giveth us shall be truly the thing he promiseth....

[12] These things considered, how should that mind which loving truth and seeking comfort out of holy mysteries hath not perhaps the leisure, perhaps not the wit nor capacity to tread out so endless mazes, as the intricate disputes of this cause have led men into, how should a virtuously disposed mind better resolve with itself than thus? "Variety of judgments and opinions argueth obscurity in those things whereabout they differ. But that which all parts receive for truth, that which every one having sifted is by no one denied or doubted of, must needs be matter of infallible certainty. Whereas therefore there are but three expositions made of 'this is my body', the first, 'this is in itself before participation *really and truly the natural substance of my body by reason of the coexistence which my omnipotent body hath with the sanctified element of bread'*, which is the Lutherans' interpretation; the second, 'this is itself and before participation *the very true and natural substance of my body, by force of that Deity which with the words of consecration abolisheth the substance of bread and substituteth in the place thereof my Body'*, which is the popish construction; the last, '*this hallowed food, through concurrence of divine power, is in verity and truth, unto faithful receivers, instrumentally a cause of that mystical participation, whereby as I make myself wholly theirs, so I give them in hand an actual possession of all such saving grace as my sacrificed body can yield, and as their souls do presently need, this is* to them and in them *my body'*: of these three rehearsed interpretations the last hath in it nothing but what the rest do all approve and acknowledge to be most true, nothing but that which the words of Christ are on all sides confessed to enforce, nothing but that which the Church of God hath always thought necessary, nothing but that which alone is sufficient for every Christian man to believe concerning the use and force of this sacrament, finally nothing but that wherewith the writings of all antiquity are consonant and all Christian confessions agreeable. And as truth in what kind soever is by no kind of truth gainsayed, so the mind which resteth itself on this is never troubled with those perplexities which the other do both

find, by means of so great contradiction between their opinions and true principles of reason grounded upon experience, nature and sense. Which albeit with boisterous courage and breath they seem oftentimes to blow away, yet whoso observeth how again they labour and sweat by subtlety of wit to make some show of agreement between their peculiar conceits and the general edicts of nature, must needs perceive they struggle with that which they cannot fully master. Besides sith of that which is proper to themselves their discourses are hungry and unpleasant, full of tedious and irksome labour, heartless and hitherto without fruit, on the other side read we them or hear we others be they of our own or of ancienter times, to what part soever they be thought to incline touching that whereof there is controversy, yet in this where they all speak but one thing their discourses are heavenly, their words sweet as the honeycomb, their tongues melodiously tuned instruments, their sentences mere consolation and joy, are we not hereby almost even with the voice from heaven, admonished which we may safeliest cleave unto?

"He which hath said of the one sacrament, 'wash and be clean', hath said concerning the other likewise, 'eat and live'. If therefore without any such particular and solemn warrant as this is that poor distressed woman coming unto Christ for health could so constantly resolve herself, 'may I but touch the skirt of his garment I shall be whole' [Matthew, ix.21], what moveth us to argue of the manner how life should come by bread, our duty being here but to take what is offered, and most assuredly to rest persuaded of this, that can we but eat we are safe? When I behold with mine eyes some small and scarce discernible grain or seed whereof nature maketh promise that a tree shall come, and when afterwards of that tree any skilful artificer undertaketh to frame some exquisite and curious work, I look for the event, I move no question about performance either of the one or of the other. Shall I simply credit nature in things natural, shall I in things artificial rely myself on art, never offering to make doubt, and in that which is above both art and nature refuse to believe the author of both, except he acquaint me with his ways, and lay the secret of his skill before me? Where God himself doth speak those

things which either for height and sublimity of matter, or else
for secresy of performance we are not able to reach unto, as we
may be ignorant without danger, so it can be no disgrace to confess we are ignorant. Such as love piety will as much as in them
lieth know all things that God commandeth, but especially the
duties of service which they owe to God. As for his dark and
hidden works, they prefer as becometh them in such cases
simplicity of faith before that knowledge, which curiously sifting
what it should adore, and disputing too boldly of that which the
wit of man cannot search, chilleth for the most part all warmth
of zeal, and bringeth soundness of belief many times into great
hazard. Let it therefore be sufficient for me presenting myself at
the Lord's table to know what there I receive from him, without
searching or inquiring of the manner how Christ performeth his
promise; let disputes and questions, enemies to piety, abate-
ments of true devotion, and hitherto in this cause but over
patiently heard, let them take their rest; let curious and sharp-
witted men beat their heads about what questions themselves
will, the very letter of the word of Christ giveth plain security
that these mysteries do as nails fasten us to his very Cross, that
by them we draw out, as touching efficacy, force, and virtue,
even the blood of his gored side, in the wounds of our Redeemer
we there dip our tongues, we are dyed red both within and without, our hunger is satisfied and our thirst for ever quenched; they
are things wonderful which he feeleth, great which he seeth and
unheard of which he uttereth, whose soul is possessed of this
Paschal Lamb and made joyful in the strength of this new wine,
this bread hath in it more than the substance which our eyes
behold, this cup hallowed with solemn benediction availeth to
the endless life and welfare both of soul and body, in that it
serveth as well for a medicine to heal our infirmities and purge
our sins as for a sacrifice of thanksgiving; with touching it
sanctifieth, it enlighteneth with belief, it truly conformeth us unto
the image of Jesus Christ; what these elements are in themselves
it skilleth not, it is enough that to me which take them they are
the body and blood of Christ, his promise in witness hereof
sufficeth, his word he knoweth which way to accomplish; why

should any cogitation possess the mind of a faithful communicant but this, O my God thou art true, O my Soul thou art happy!"

(V.lxvii.1-7, 12)

54   DANGERS OF EXCESSIVE REFORM

... Whereas they which do all profess the Christian religion are divided amongst themselves, and the fault of the one part is that in zeal to the sufferings of Christ they admire too much and over-superstitiously adore the visible sign of his Cross, if you ask what we that mislike them should do, we are here advised to cure one contrary by another. Which art or method is not yet so current as they imagine.

For if, as their practice for the most part sheweth, it be their meaning that the scope and drift of reformation when things are faulty should be to *settle* the Church in the contrary, it standeth them upon to beware of this rule, because seeing vices have not only virtues but other vices also in nature opposite unto them, it may be dangerous in these cases to seek but that which we find contrary to present evils. For in sores and sicknesses of the mind we are not simply to measure good by distance from evil, because one vice may in some respect be more opposite to another than either of them to that virtue which holdeth the mean between them both. Liberality and covetousness, the one a virtue and the other a vice, are not so contrary as the vices of covetousness and prodigality; religion and superstition have more affiance, though the one be light and the other darkness, than superstition and profaneness which both are vicious extremities. By means whereof it cometh also to pass that the mean which is virtue seemeth in the eyes of each extreme an extremity; the liberal hearted man is by the opinion of the prodigal miserable, and by the judgment of the miserable lavish; impiety for the most part upbraideth religion as superstitious, which superstition often accuseth as impious, both so conceiving thereof because it doth seem more to participate each extreme, than one extreme doth another, and is by consequent less contrary to either of them, than they mutually between themselves. Now if he that seeketh to reform covetousness or superstition should but labour to induce the contrary, it were but to draw men out of lime into coaldust. So that their course which will remedy the superstitious abuse of things profitable in the Church is not still to abolish utterly the use thereof, because not using at all is most opposite to ill using, but rather if it may be to bring them back to a right perfect and religious usage, which albeit less contrary to the present sore is notwithstanding the better and by many degrees the sounder way of recovery.   (V.lxv.20)

55   GLORY OF THE PRIESTLY VOCATION

LXXVII. The ministry of things divine is a function which as God did himself institute, so neither may men undertake the same but by authority and power given them in lawful manner. That God which is no way deficient or wanting unto man in necessaries, and hath therefore given us the light of his heavenly truth, because without that inestimable benefit we must needs have wandered in darkness to our endless perdition and woe, hath in the like abundance of mercies ordained certain to attend upon the due execution of requisite parts and offices therein prescribed for the good of the whole world, which men thereunto assigned do hold their authority from him, whether they be such as himself immediately or as the Church in his name investeth, it being neither possible for all nor for every man without distinction convenient to take upon him a charge of so great importance. They are therefore ministers of God, not only by way of subordination as princes and civil magistrates whose execution of judgment and justice the supreme hand of divine providence doth uphold, but ministers of God as from whom their authority is derived, and not from men. For in that they are Christ's ambassadors and his labourers, who should give them their commission but he whose most inward affairs they manage? Is not God alone the Father of spirits? Are not souls the purchase of Jesus Christ? What angel in Heaven could have said to man as our Lord did unto Peter, "Feed my sheep: Preach: Baptize: Do this in remembrance of me: Whose sins ye retain they are retained: and their offences in heaven pardoned whose faults you shall on earth forgive?" What think we? Are these terrestrial sounds, or else are they voices uttered out of the clouds above? The power of the ministry of God translateth out of darkness into glory, it raiseth men from the earth and bringeth God himself down from heaven, by blessing visible elements it maketh them invisible grace, it giveth daily the Holy Ghost, it hath to dispose of that flesh which was given for the life of the world and that blood which was poured out to redeem souls, when it poureth malediction upon the heads of the wicked they perish, when it revoketh the same they revive. O wretched blindness if we admire not so great power, more wretched if we consider it aright and notwithstanding imagine that any but God can bestow it!

(V.lxxvii.1)

Book VI

Book VI, supposedly to be about lay-elders, is mainly about penitence (56, 57, 58; also v.5). Book VII deals with bishops (59, 60, 61; also xviii.4-6), concluding with a defence of the temporalities of the Church (62; also xxiii.5), whilst Book VIII concerns itself with different aspects of the Royal Supremacy, arguing for the unanimity of church and state (63), divine right (a bit casuistically, be it said: 64), the simultaneity of Christ as Head of the Church invisible and the monarch of the church visible (65), and the relationship of Church and Parliament and monarch (66).

56   SPIRITUAL JURISDICTION

[2] The spiritual power of the Church being such as neither can be challenged by right of nature, nor could by human authority be instituted, because the forces and effects thereof are supernatural and divine; we are to make no doubt or question, but that from him which is the Head it hath descended unto us that are the body now invested therewith. He gave it for the benefit and good of souls, as a mean to keep them in the path which leadeth unto endless felicity, a bridle to hold them within their due and convenient bounds, and if they do go astray, a forcible help to reclaim them. Now although there be no kind of spiritual power, for which our Lord Jesus Christ did not give both commission to exercise, and direction how to use the same, although his laws in that behalf recorded by the holy evangelists be the only ground and foundation, whereupon the practice of the Church must sustain itself: yet, as all multitudes, once grown to the form of societies, are even thereby naturally warranted to enforce upon their own subjects particularly those things which public wisdom shall judge expedient for the common good: so it were absurd to imagine the Church itself, the most glorious amongst them, abridged of this liberty; or to think that no law, constitution, or canon, can be further made either for limitation or amplification in the practice of our Saviour's ordinances, whatsoever occasion

be offered through variety of times and things, during the state of this unconstant world, which bringing forth daily such new evils as must of necessity by new remedies be redrest, did both of old enforce our venerable predecessors, and will always constrain others, sometime to make, sometime to abrogate, sometime to augment, and again to abridge sometime; in sum often to vary, alter, and change customs incident into the manner of exercising that power which doth itself continue always one and the same. I therefore conclude, that spiritual authority is a power which Christ hath given to be used over them which are subject unto it for the eternal good of their souls, according to his own most sacred laws and the wholesome positive constitutions of his Church.
                                                                    (VI.ii.2)

57 PENITENCE

III. Seeing then that the chiefest cause of spiritual jurisdiction is to provide for the health and safety of men's souls, by bringing them to see and repent their grievous offences committed against God, as also to reform all injuries offered with the breach of Christian love and charity, towards their brethren, in matters of ecclesiastical cognizance; the use of this power shall by so much the plainlier appear, if first the nature of repentance itself be known.

We are by repentance to appease whom we offend by sin. For which cause, whereas all sins deprive us of the favour of Almighty God, our way of reconciliation with him is the inward secret repentance of the heart; which inward repentance alone sufficeth, unless some special thing, in the quality of sin committed, or in the party that hath done amiss, require more. For besides our submission in God's sight, repentance must not only proceed to the private contentation of men, if the sin be a crime injurious; but also further, where the wholesome discipline of God's Church exacteth a more exemplary and open satisfaction. Now the Church being satisfied with outward repentance, as God is with inward, it shall not be amiss, for more perspicuity, to term this latter always the Virtue, that former the Discipline of Repentance: which discipline hath two sorts of penitents to work upon, inasmuch as it hath been accustomed to lay the offices of repentance on some seeking, others shunning them; on some at their own voluntary request, on others altogether against their wills; as shall hereafter appear by store of ancient examples. Repentance being therefore either in the sight of God alone, or else with the notice also of men: without the one, sometimes throughly performed, but always practised more or less, in our daily devotions and prayers, we have no remedy for any fault; whereas the other is only required in sins of a certain degree and quality: the one necessary for ever, the other so far forth as the laws and orders of God's Church shall make it requisite: the nature, parts, and effects of the one always the same; the other limited, extended, varied by infinite occasions.

[2] The virtue of repentance in the heart of man is God's handy work, a fruit or effect of divine grace. Which grace continually offereth itself, even unto them that have forsaken it, as may appear by the words of Christ in St. John's Revelation [iii.20], "I stand at the door and knock" nor doth he only knock without, but also within assist to open, whereby access and entrance is given to the heavenly presence of that saving power, which maketh man a repaired Temple for God's good Spirit again to inhabit. And albeit the whole train of virtues which are implied in the name of grace be infused at one instant; yet because when they meet and concur unto any effect in man, they have their distinct operations rising orderly one from another; it is no unnecessary thing that we note the way or method of the Holy Ghost in framing man's sinful heart to repentance....

[3] The root and beginning of penitency therefore is the consideration of our own sin, as a cause which hath procured the wrath, and a subject which doth need the mercy of God. For unto man's understanding there being presented, on the one side, tribulation and anguish upon every soul that doth evil; on the other, eternal life unto them which by continuance in well-doing seek glory, and honour, and immortality: on the one hand, a curse to the

children of disobedience; on the other, to lovers of righteousness all grace and benediction: yet between these extremes, that eternal God, from whose unspotted justice and undeserved mercy the lot of each inheritance proceedeth, is so inclinable rather to shew compassion than to take revenge, that all his speeches in Holy Scripture are almost nothing else but entreaties of men to prevent destruction by amendment of their wicked lives; all the works of his providence little other than mere allurements of the just to continue steadfast, and of the unrighteous to change their course; all his dealings and proceedings such towards true converts, as have even filled the grave writings of holy men with these and the like most sweet sentences: "Repentance (if I may so speak) stoppeth God in his way, when being provoked by crimes past he cometh to revenge them with most just punishments; yea, it tieth as it were the hands of the avenger, and doth not suffer him to have his will" [Cassian]. Again, "The merciful eye of God towards men hath no power to withstand penitency, at what time soever it comes in presence". And again, "God doth not take it so in evil part, though we wound that which he hath required us to keep whole, as that after we have taken hurt there should be in us no desire to receive his help" [Basil]. Finally, lest I be carried too far in so large a sea, "There was never any man condemned of God but for neglect, nor justified except he had care, of repentance" [Fulgentius].

[5] Now in a penitent's or convert's duty, there are included, first, the aversion of the will from sin; secondly, the submission of ourselves to God by supplication and prayer; thirdly, the purpose of a new life, testified with present works of amendment: which three things do very well seem to be comprised in one definition, by them which handle repentance, as a virtue that hateth, bewaileth, and sheweth a purpose to amend sin. We offend God in thought, word, and deed. To the first of which three, they make contrition; to the second, confession; and to the last, our works of satisfaction, answerable.

Contrition doth not here import those sudden pangs and convulsions of the mind which cause sometimes the most forsaken of God to retract their own doings; it is no natural passion or anguish, which riseth in us against our wills, but a deliberate aversion of the will of man from sin; which being always accompanied with grief, and grief oftentimes partly with tears, partly with other external signs, it hath been thought, that in these things contrition doth chiefly consist: whereas the chiefest thing in contrition is that alteration whereby the will, which was before delighted with sin, doth now abhor and shun nothing more. But forasmuch as we cannot hate sin in ourselves without heaviness and grief, that there should be in us a thing of such hateful quality, the will averted from sin must needs make the affection suitable; yea, great reason why it should so do: for sith the will by conceiving sin hath deprived the soul of life; and of life there is no recovery without repentance, the death of sin; repentance not able to kill sin, but by withdrawing the will from it; the will unpossible to be withdrawn, unless it concur with a contrary affection to that which accompanied it before in evil: is it not clear that as an inordinate delight did first begin sin, so repentance must begin with a just sorrow, a sorrow of heart, and such a sorrow as renteth the heart; neither a feigned nor a slight sorrow; not feigned, lest it increase sin; nor slight, lest the pleasures of sin overmatch it.

(VI.iii.1-3, 5)

58   CONFESSION IN THE CHURCH OF ENGLAND

[15] It standeth with us in the Church of England, as touching public confession, thus:

First, seeing day by day we in our Church begin our public prayers to Almighty God with public acknowledgment of our sins, in which confession every man prostrate as it were before his glorious Majesty crieth guilty against himself; and the minister with one sentence pronounceth universally all clear, whose acknowledgment so made hath proceeded from a true penitent mind; what reason is there every man should not under the general terms of confession represent to himself his own particulars whatsoever, and adjoining thereunto that affection which a contrite spirit worketh, embrace to as full effect the words of divine Grace, as if the same were severally and particularly uttered with addition of prayers, imposition of hands, or all the ceremonies and solemnities that might be used for the strengthening of man's affiance in God's peculiar mercy towards them? Such complements are helps to support our weakness, and not causes that serve to procure or produce his gifts. If with us there be "truth in the inward parts", as David speaketh, the difference of general and particular forms in confession and absolution is not so material, that any man's safety or ghostly good should depend upon it.

And for private confession and absolution it standeth thus with us:

The minister's power to absolve is publicly taught and professed, the Church not denied to have authority either of abridging or enlarging the use and exercise of that power, upon the people no such necessity imposed of opening their transgressions unto men, as if remission of sins otherwise were impossible; neither any such opinion had of the thing itself, as though it were either unlawful or unprofitable, saving only for these inconveniences, which the world hath by experience observed in it heretofore. And in regard thereof, the Church of England hitherto hath thought it the safer way to refer men's hidden crimes unto God and themselves only; howbeit, not without special caution for the admonition of such as come to the holy Sacrament, and for the comfort of such as are ready to depart the world.

(VI.iv.15)

Book VII

59 THE OFFICE OF A BISHOP

A Bishop is a minister of God, unto whom with permanent continuance there is given not only power of administering the Word and Sacraments, which power other Presbyters have; but also a further power to ordain ecclesiastical persons, and a power of chiefty in government over Presbyters as well as Laymen, a power to be by way of jurisdiction a Pastor even to Pastors themselves. So that this office, as he is a Presbyter or Pastor, consisteth in those things which are common unto him with other pastors, as in ministering the Word and Sacraments: but those things incident unto his office, which do properly make him a Bishop, cannot be common unto him with other Pastors.

(VII.ii.3)

60 VALUE OF EPISCOPAL AUTHORITY

[3] Bishops we say there have been always, even as long as the Church of Christ itself hath been. The Apostles who planted it, did themselves rule as bishops over it; neither could they so well have kept things in order during their own times, but that episcopal authority was given them from above, to exercise far and wide over all other guides and pastors of God's Church. The Church indeed for a time continued without bishops by restraint, every where established in Christian cities. But shall we thereby conclude that the Church hath no use of them, that without them it may stand and flourish? No, the cause wherefore they were so soon universally appointed was, for that it plainly appeared that without them the Church could not have continued long. It was by the special providence of God no doubt so disposed, that the evil whereof this did serve for remedy might first be felt, and so the reverend authority of bishops be made by so much the more

effectual, when our general experience had taught men what it was for churches to want them. Good laws are never esteemed so good, nor acknowledged so necessary, as when precedent crimes are as seeds out of which they grow. Episcopal authority was even in a manner sanctified unto the Church of Christ by that little bitter experience which it first had of the pestilent evil of schisms. Again, when this very thing was proposed as a remedy, yet a more suspicious and fearful acceptance it must needs have found, if the selfsame provident wisdom of Almighty God had not also given beforehand sufficient trial thereof in the regiment of Jerusalem, a mother church, which having received the same order even at the first, was by it most peaceably governed, when other churches without it had trouble. So that by all means the necessary use of episcopal government is confirmed, yea strengthened it is and ratified, even by the not establishment thereof in all churches every where at the first. . . .

[4] Thus we see that prelacy must needs be acknowledged exceedingly beneficial in the Church; and yet for more perspicuity's sake, it shall not be pains superfluously taken, if the manner how be also declared at large. For this one thing not understood by the vulgar sort, causeth all contempt to be offered unto higher powers, not only ecclesiastical, but civil: whom when proud men have disgraced, and are therefore reproved by such as carry some dutiful affection of mind, the usual apologies which they make for themselves are these: "What more virtue in these great ones than in others? We see no such eminent good which they do above other men".

We grant indeed, that the good which higher governors do is not so immediate and near unto every of us, as many times the meaner labours of others under them, and this doth make it to be less esteemed. But we must note, that it is in this case as in a ship; he that sitteth at the stern is quiet, he moveth not, he seemeth in a manner to do little or nothing in comparison of them that sweat about other toil, yet that which he doth is in value and force more than all the labours of the residue laid together. The influence of the heavens above worketh infinitely more to our good, and yet appeareth not half so sensible as the force doth of things below. We consider not what it is which we reap by the authority of our chiefest spiritual governors, nor are likely to enter into any consideration thereof, till we want them; and that is the cause why they are at our hands so unthankfully rewarded.

[5] Authority is a constraining power, which power were needless if we were all such as we should be, willing to do the things we ought to do without constraint. But because generally we are otherwise, therefore we all reap singular benefit by that authority which permitteth no men, though they would, to slack their duty. It doth not suffice, that the lord of an household appoint labourers what they should do, unless he set over them some chief workmen to see that they do it. Constitutions and canons made for the ordering of church affairs are dead taskmasters. The due execution of laws spiritual dependeth most upon the vigilant care of the chiefest spiritual governors, whose charge is to see that such laws be kept by the clergy and people under them: with those duties which the law of God and the ecclesiastical canons require in the clergy, lay governors are neither for the most part so well acquainted, nor so deeply and nearly touched. Requisite therefore it is, that ecclesiastical persons have authority in such things; which kind of authority maketh them that have it prelates. If then it be a thing confessed, as by all good men it needs must be, to have prayers read in all churches, to have the sacraments of God administered, to have the mysteries of salvation painfully taught, to have God every where devoutly worshipped, and all this perpetually, and with quietness, bringeth unto the whole Church, and unto every member thereof, inestimable good; how can that authority which hath been proved the ordinance of God for preservation of these duties in the Church, how can it choose but deserve to be held a thing publicly most beneficial?

[6] It were to be wished, and is to be laboured for, as much as can be, that they who are set in such rooms may be furnished with honourable qualities and graces, every way fit for their calling: but be they otherwise, howsoever, so long as they are in authority, all men reap some good by them, albeit not so much good as if they were abler men. There is not amongst us all, but

is a great deal more apt to exact another man's duty, than the best of us is to discharge exactly his own; and therefore prelates, although neglecting many ways their duty unto God and men, do notwithstanding by their authority great good, in that they keep others at the leastwise in some awe under them. It is our duty therefore in this consideration, to honour them that rule as prelates; which office if they discharge it well, the Apostle's own verdict is, that the honour they have they be worthy of, yea though it were double [1 Tim. v.17]. And if their government be otherwise, the judgment of sage men hath ever been this, that albeit the dealings of governors be culpable, yet honourable they must be, in respect of that Authority by which they govern. Great caution must be used that we neither be emboldened to follow them in evil, whom for authority's sake we honour; nor induced in authority to dishonour them, whom as examples we may not follow. In a word, not to dislike sin, though it should be in the highest, were unrighteous meekness; and proud righteousness it is to contemn or dishonour highness, though it should be in the sinfullest men that live.   (VII.xiii.3; xviii.4-6)

61   EPISCOPAL SUCCESSION

[11] Now whereas hereupon some do infer, that no ordination can stand but only such as is made by bishops, which have had their ordination likewise by other bishops before them, till we come to the very Apostles of Christ themselves; in which respect it was demanded of Beza at Poissie [1561], "By what authority he could administer the holy sacraments, being not thereunto ordained by any other than Calvin, or by such as to whom the power of ordination did not belong, according to the ancient orders and customs of the Church; sith Calvin and they who joined with him in that action were no bishops": and Athanasius maintaineth the fact of Macarius a presbyter, which overthrew the holy table whereat one Ischyras would have ministered the blessed Sacrament, having not been consecrated thereunto by

laying on of some bishop's hands, according to the ecclesiastical canons; as also Epiphanius inveigheth sharply against divers for doing the like, when they had not episcopal ordination: to this we answer, that there may be sometimes very just and sufficient reason to allow ordination made without a bishop.

The whole Church visible being the true original subject of all power, it hath not ordinarily allowed any other than bishops alone to ordain: howbeit, as the ordinary course is ordinarily in all things to be observed, so it may be in some cases not unnecessary that we decline from the ordinary ways.

Men may be extraordinarily, yet allowably, two ways admitted unto spiritual functions in the Church. One is, when God himself doth of himself raise up any, whose labour he useth without requiring that men should authorize them; but then he doth ratify their calling by manifest signs and tokens himself from heaven: and thus even such as believed not our Saviour's teaching, did yet acknowledge him a lawful teacher sent from God: "Thou art a teacher sent from God, otherwise none could do those things which thou doest" [John iii.2]. Luther did but reasonably therefore, in declaring that the senate of Mulheuse should do well to ask of Muncer, from whence he received power to teach, who it was that had called him; and if his answer were that God had given him his charge, then to require at his hands some evident sign thereof for men's satisfaction: because so God is wont, when he himself is the author of any extraordinary calling.

Another extraordinary kind of vocation is, when the exigence of necessity doth constrain to leave the usual ways of the Church, which otherwise we would willingly keep: where the church must needs have some ordained, and neither hath nor can have possibly a bishop to ordain; in case of such necessity, the ordinary institution of God hath given oftentimes, and may give, place. And therefore we are not simply without exception to urge a lineal descent of power from the Apostles by continued succession of bishops in every effectual ordination. These cases of inevitable necessity excepted, none may ordain but only bishops: by the imposition of their hands it is, that the Church giveth power of order, both unto presbyters and deacons.   [VII.xiv.11)

62 CHURCH PROPERTY – GOD'S PROPERTY

XXII. Possessions, lands and livings spiritual, the wealth of the clergy, the goods of the Church, are in such sort the Lord's own, that man can challenge no propriety in them. His they are, and not ours; all things are his, in that from him they have their being. "My corn, and my wine, and mine oil", saith the Lord [Hosea ii.8]. All things his, in that he hath absolute power to dispose of them at his pleasure. "Mine (saith he) are the sheep and oxen of a thousand hills" [Psalm l.10]. All things his, in that when we have them, we may say with Job, "God hath given"; and when we are deprived of them, "The Lord", whose they are, hath likewise "taken them away" again [Job i.21]. But these sacred possessions are his by another tenure; his, because those men who first received them from him have unto him returned them again by way of religious gift or oblation: and in this respect it is, that the Lord doth term those houses wherein such gifts and oblations were laid, "his treasuries" [Malachi iii.10].

(VII.xxii.1)

Book VIII

63 CHURCH OF ENGLAND'S UNIVERSAL
CURE OF SOULS

With us therefore the name of a church importeth only a society of men, first united into some public form of regiment, and secondly distinguished from other societies by the exercise of Christian religion. With them on the other side the name of the Church in this present question importeth not only a multitude of men so united and so distinguished, but also further the same divided necessarily and perpetually from the body of the commonwealth: so that even in such a politic society as consisteth of none but Christians, yet the Church of Christ and the commonwealth are two corporations, independently each subsisting by itself.

We hold, that seeing there is not any man of the Church of England but the same man is also a member of the commonwealth; nor any man a member of the commonwealth, which is not also of the Church of England; therefore as in a figure triangular the base doth differ from the sides thereof, and yet one and the selfsame line is both a base and also a side; a side simply, a base if it chance to be the bottom and underlie the rest: so, albeit properties and actions of one kind do cause the name of a commonwealth, qualities and functions of another sort the name of a Church to be given unto a multitude, yet one and the selfsame multitude may in such sort be both, and is so with us, that no person appertaining to the one can be denied to be also of the other. Contrariwise, unless they against us should hold, that the Church and the commonwealth are two, both distinct and separate societies, of which two, the one comprehendeth always persons not belonging to the other; that which they do they could not conclude out of the difference between the Church and the commonwealth; namely, that bishops may not meddle with the affairs of the commonwealth, because they are governors of another corporation, which is the Church; nor kings with making laws for the Church, because they have government not of this

191

corporation, but of another divided from it, the commonwealth; and the walls of separation between these two must for ever be upheld. They hold the necessity of personal separation, which clean excludeth the power of one man's dealing in both; we of natural, which doth not hinder but that one and the same person may in both bear a principal sway. (VIII.1.2)

64   DEFENCE OF DIVINE RIGHT

[6] Again, on whom the same is bestowed even at men's discretion, they likewise do hold it by divine right. If God in his own revealed word have appointed such power to be, although himself extraordinarily bestow it not, but leave the appointment of the persons unto men; yea, albeit God do neither appoint the thing nor assign the person; nevertheless when men have established both, who doth doubt but that sundry duties and offices depending thereupon are prescribed in the word of God, and consequently by that very right to be exacted?

For example's sake, the power which the Roman emperors had over foreign provinces was not a thing which the law of God did ever institute, neither was Tiberius Cæsar by special commission from heaven therewith invested; and yet the payment of tribute unto Cæsar being made emperor is the plain law of Jesus Christ. Unto kings by human right, honour by very divine right, is due; man's ordinances are many times presupposed as grounds in the statutes of God. And therefore of what kind soever the means be whereby governors are lawfully advanced unto their seats, as we by the law of God stand bound meekly to acknowledge them for God's lieutenants, and to confess their power his, so they by the same law are both authorized and required to use that power as far as it may be in any sort available to his honour.

(VIII.ii.6)

65   SPIRITUAL AND TEMPORAL GOVERNMENT
OF THE CHURCH

To make things therefore so plain that henceforth a child's capacity may serve rightly to conceive our meaning: we make the spiritual regiment of Christ to be generally that whereby his Church is ruled and governed in things spiritual. Of this general we make two distinct kinds; the one invisibly exercised by Christ himself in his own person; the other outwardly administered by them whom Christ doth allow to be the rulers and guiders of his Church. Touching the former of these two kinds, we teach that Christ in regard thereof is peculiarly termed the Head of the Church of God; neither can any other creature in that sense and meaning be termed head besides him, because it importeth the conduct and government of our souls by the hand of that blessed Spirit wherewith we are sealed and marked, as being peculiarly his. Him only therefore we do acknowledge to be that Lord, which dwelleth, liveth and reigneth in our hearts; him only to be that Head, which giveth salvation and life unto his body; him only to be that fountain, from whence the influence of heavenly grace distilleth, and is derived into all parts, whether the word, or sacraments, or discipline, or whatsoever be the mean whereby it floweth. As for the power of administering these things in the Church of Christ, which power we call the power of order, it is indeed both Spiritual and His; Spiritual, because such duties properly concern the Spirit; His, because by him it was instituted. Howbeit neither spiritual, as that which is inwardly and invisibly exercised; nor his, as that which he himself in person doth exercise.

Again, that power of dominion which is indeed the point of this controversy, and doth also belong to the second kind of spiritual government namely unto that regiment which is external and visible; this likewise being spiritual in regard of the matter about which it dealeth, and being his, inasmuch as he approveth whatsoever is done by it, must notwithstanding be distinguished also from that power whereby he himself in person administereth the former kind of his own spiritual regiment, because he himself in person doth not administer this. We do not, therefore, vainly imagine, but truly and rightly discern a power external and visible in the Church, exercised by men, and severed in nature from that spiritual power of Christ's own regiment, which power is termed spiritual, because it worketh secretly, inwardly, and invisibly; his, because none doth or can it personally exercise, either besides or together with him. So that him only we may name our Head, in regard of this, and yet, in regard of that other power differing from this, term others also besides him heads, without any contradiction at all.   (VIII.iv.10)

66   KING, PARLIAMENT AND CHURCH

The most natural and religious course in making of laws is, that the matter of them be taken from the judgment of the wisest in those things which they are to concern. In matters of God, to set down a form of public prayer, a solemn confession of the articles of Christian faith, rites and ceremonies meet for the exercise of religion; it were unnatural not to think the pastors and bishops of our souls a great deal more fit, than men of secular trades and callings: howbeit, when all which the wisdom of all sorts can do is done for devising of laws in the Church, it is the general consent of all that giveth them the form and vigour of laws, without which they could be no more unto us than the counsels of physicians to the sick: well might they seem as wholesome admonitions and instructions, but laws could they never be without consent of the whole Church, which is the only thing that bindeth each member of the Church, to be guided by them. Whereunto both nature and the practice of the Church of God set down in Scripture, is found every way so fully consonant, that God himself would not impose, no not his own laws upon his people by the hand of Moses, without their free and open consent. Wherefore to define and determine even of the church's affairs by way of assent and approbation, as laws are defined of in that right of power, which doth give them the force of laws;

thus to define of our own church's regiment, the parliament of England hath competent authority.

Touching the supremacy of power which our kings have in this case of making laws, it resteth principally in the strength of a negative voice; which not to give them, were to deny them that without which they were but kings by mere title, and not in exercise of dominion. Be it in states of regiment popular, aristocratical, or regal, principality resteth in that person, or those persons, unto whom is given the right of excluding any kind of law whatsoever it be before establishment.   (VIII.vi.11)

Glossary of Names

Ambrose (c.339-397) Bishop of Milan.

Anabaptists denounced the baptism of infants, believed in a church exclusively of the allegedly converted and supported the separation of church and state.

Arians believed that Christ was created by and not co-eternal with God the Father.

Aristotle (384-322 BC) Greek philosopher and encyclopaedic writer.

Athanasius (c.296-373) champion of orthodoxy against Arianism.

Augustine (354-430) Bishop of Hippo (North Africa), famous for his *Confessions* and his massive treatise *The City of God*, a defence of Christianity and refutation of pagan mythology.

Basil (329-375) Bishop of Caesarea and voluminous writer. His *De Spiritu Sancto* was a defence against accusations of unsound doctrine on the Trinity.

Beza, Theodore (1519-1605) Calvin's successor at Geneva. The Colloquy of Poissy at which Beza represented the French Protestants took place in 1561.

Boethius (d.524) author of the *Consolation of Philosophy*, which finds in God the highest good and only source of true happiness.

Cartwright, Thomas (1535-1603) leading Puritan divine, Professor of Divinity at Cambridge (1569) but deposed. Spent some time in Geneva and other continental centres of Calvinistic inclination.

Cassian, John (d.c.430) ascetic writer of the *Institutes*, and institutor of several monasteries in southern France.

Cicero, Marcus Tullius (109-43 BC) Roman orator and writer.

Clement (*c*.155-*c*.220) of Alexandria, first known Christian scholar, writing against Gnostic heresy.

Cyprian (*c*.200-258) Bishop of Carthage, mainly memorable as a pastor and administrator rather than as a theologian.

Damascene, John (*c*.675-*c*.749) Greek theologian, last of the great Eastern fathers of the Church.

Donatists were adherents of a separatist African church of the fourth century, characterized by moral rigour, puritan beliefs in church order, and rejection of the state and society.

Duns Scotus (1266-1308) scholastic theologian, who claimed that faith was a matter of will not supportable by logical proofs.

Epiphanius (*c*.315-403) Bishop of Salamis, rigorously orthodox.

Fulgentius (468-533) Bishop of Ruspe, ascetic and devotee of St. Augustine.

Galen (130-?167) Roman physician and voluminous writer on medical subjects. Admirer of Hippocrates.

Gregory of Nazianzus (330-389) friend of Basil, wrote against the Arians after being summoned from monastic retreat.

Hippocrates (460-357 BC) celebrated Greek medical writer, called the "Father of Medicine".

Irenaeus (*fl*.175-195) Bishop of Lyons, wrote against the Gnostics who devalued the redemptive status of Christ.

Jerome (*c*.345-*c*.419) Biblical translator and voluminous theological controversialist.

Justinian (483-565) Emperor, codified the Roman legal system.

Lactantius (*c*.240-*c*.320) Christian apologist, noted for his lucidity and style.

Munzer, Thomas (d.1525) radical and inflammatory preacher. Helped to organize the Peasants' Revolt at Mulhausen, and was executed for his role in this uprising. Originally a follower of Luther.

Œcolampadius (1482-1531) German reformer, friend of Zwingli.

Plato (428-348 BC) Greek philosopher of idealistic views, claiming that all knowledge rests on eternal principles and is not derived from experience.

Pythagoras (584-504 BC) Greek philosopher whose theory, according to Aristotle, was based on the relationship of numbers.

Sophocles (c.496-406 BC) Greek tragic dramatist.

Strabo (66 BC-24 AD) Roman traveller and geographer.

Tertullian (c.160-c.215) African moralist and theologian of extreme and rigorous views.

Theophrastus (c.370-287 BC) prolific writer on many subjects. A great deal of his work has been lost, the best-known of what remains being his study of different temperaments and personalities, *Characters*.

Whitaker, William (1548-1595) Puritan theologian. Professor of Divinity at Cambridge (1580), later Master of St John's and Trinity Colleges.

Zwingli, Ulrich (1484-1531) Swiss reformer, known for his memorialist view of the Eucharist.